CRAIES ON LEGISLATION

SECOND SUPPLEMENT TO THE TENTH EDITION

CRAIES ON LEGISLATION

SECOND SUPPLEMENT TO THE TENTH EDITION

by

Daniel Greenberg
Barrister; Parliamentary Counsel, Berwin Leighton Paisner LLP

SWEET & MAXWELL

THOMSON REUTERS

Published in 2015 by Thomson Reuters (Professional) UK Limited
trading as Sweet & Maxwell, Friars House,
160 Blackfriars Road, London, SE1 8EZ
(Registered in England & Wales, Company No 1679046.
Registered Office and address for service:
2nd Floor, 1 Mark Square, Leonard Street, London EC2A 4EG)

For further information on our products and services, visit
www.sweetandmaxwell.co.uk

Typeset by Wright and Round Ltd., Gloucester
Printed in Great Britain by Ashford Colour Press, Gosport, Hants

No natural forests were destroyed to make this product; only farmed
timber was used and re-planted.

A CIP catalogue record for this book is available from the British Library.

ISBN 978 0 414 05113 3

HOW TO USE THIS SUPPLEMENT

The second supplement to the 10th edn of *Craies on Legislation* is ordered according to the structure of the main volume.

At the beginning of the supplementary coverage for each chapter, the mini table of contents from the main volume has been included. Where a heading in each table of contents has been marked with a white square pointer, this material has been updated in this supplement. Any headings marked with a black square were updated in the previous 1st supplement to the 10th edn of *Craies*.

Within each chapter updating information is referenced to the relevant paragraph in the main volume. The headings that appear in the supplement should be used as a reference to indicate where the updating information relates to the material in the main volume. The instructions in the square brackets explain how the added material relates to the main volume.

PREFACE TO THE FIRST SUPPLEMENT

This first supplement to the 10th edn is being published only a year after the Edition itself, rather than after the usual two-year interval.

There are a number of reasons for this, but a particular advantage that it brings is the ability to include updated information about the position of devolved legislation in Wales, since the referendum commencing the provisions allowing the National Assembly to pass Acts.

Apart from that significant addition, this supplement includes a number of updates throughout the volume to reflect recent developments.

For the parliamentary procedure updates I am enormously grateful to Alan Sandall, formerly of the Public Bill Office, House of Commons. For assistance with the material on Welsh devolution I am enormously grateful to my son, Yisroel Greenberg.

Comments and suggestions are always most welcome and can be sent to the publishers or direct to me.

Daniel Greenberg
London
August 2013

PREFACE TO THE SECOND SUPPLEMENT

This supplement is cumulative, adding to the first supplement to the 10th edn, reflecting developments since August 2013.

Comments and suggestions are always most welcome and can be sent to the publishers or direct to me.

Daniel Greenberg
London
March 2015

CONTENTS

APPENDICES
EXTRACTS AND APPENDIX

TABLE OF CASES

TABLE OF STATUTES

*[Paragraphs in **bold** type donate where text of a section is printed.]*

TABLE OF STATUTORY INSTRUMENTS

CONCEPTS AND CLASSES

SECTION 1A

QUALITY OF LEGISLATION

[New section]   **1.1A.1**

The Political and Constitutional Reform Select Committee of the House of Commons conducted an inquiry into the quality of legislation and produced its First Report of Session 2013–14 entitled *Ensuring standards in the quality of legislation*.[34a]

The inquiry was one of the most significant general inquiries in relation to the   **1.1A.2**
quality of legislation and the problems affecting it since the Renton Report.[34b]
Rather depressingly, the two inquiries and reports consider a very similar range of issues, in a way which suggests that little or no progress has been made on many of them in the 40 years between the two Reports.[34c]

The report makes five key recommendations: **1.1A.3**

    i. that there should be a Code of Legislative Standards for good quality legislation agreed between Parliament and the Government;

[34a] May 20, 2013; HC 85.

[34b] The Preparation of Legislation, Report of a Committee appointed by the Lord President of the Council, chaired by the Rt Hon Sir (later Lord) David Renton, May 1975, Cmnd. 6053.

[34c] For example, Renton was concerned about the sheer volume of legislation as one of the principal difficulties (Ch.VII) and so was the Select Committee (Ch.2); Renton considered a range of views on the use of purpose clauses and decided that they can be helpful but should be used selectively and with caution (para.11.8), and the Select Committee considered more or less the same range of views and appear to reach a similar conclusion (para.68).

ii. that a Joint Legislative Standards Committee with an oversight role should be created;

iii. that a week should elapse between the conclusion of Public Bill Committee evidence sessions and the start of line-by-line scrutiny, to allow Members enough time to consider the evidence they have heard, and for amendments to be drafted and selected for debate;

iv. that a test for identifying constitutional legislation should be agreed between Parliament and the Government;

v. that the Government should publish the reasons why a bill has not been published in draft and cannot therefore be subject to pre-legislative scrutiny.

1.1A.4   The Government's response to the Committee's Report was published by the House of Commons in July 2013.[34d] In particular, the Government rejects the recommendations for the promulgation of a Code of Legislative Standards and for the establishment of a Legislative Standards Committee.

1.1A.5   The Committee had heard a range of evidence from Government and non-Government sources expressing concerns that the Code and Committee could have created a box-ticking culture that would have been a substitute for real and effective concern about legislative quality. What will matter will be whether the concerns addressed by the Committee are carried forward into everyday legislative scrutiny, rather than being marginalised into a particular series of Committee proceedings by reference to a Code.

SECTION 2

VOLUME OF LEGISLATION

1.2.2   The Political and Constitutional Reform Select Committee of the House of Commons' Report *Ensuring standards in the quality of legislation*[36a] notes that "A concern of many of our witnesses was the increasing volume of legislation".[36b] The key finding of the Report was that although the number of Acts has not increased, the number of pages per Act has increased significantly. The Report concentrated on the volume of primary legislation, which tends to be the primary focus of parliamentarians; but since secondary legislation is generally what controls everyday activities of individuals and businesses at a practical level, more than the high-level primary legislation under which it is made, the

---

[34d] HC 611, July 18, 2013.
[36a] May 20, 2013; HC 85.
[36b] p.7.

volume of secondary legislation is a key indicator of increasing or diminishing legislative burden.[36c]

SECTION 3

PRIMARY AND SUBORDINATE LEGISLATION

Amendment of primary legislation by secondary legislation

[New paragraph]   **1.3.14**

The principle of Henry VIII clauses is not only controversial in political terms: the courts also approach Henry VIII clauses with a presumption that amounts almost to suspicion, for reasons that they have articulated in the following terms[95a]:

> "18. The purpose of the requirement that the statute which purports to confer a power to amend primary legislation by delegated legislation should use clear words is obvious. Parliament should be told, in clear terms, if the executive intends to amend primary legislation. As Lord Hoffmann observed, in the context of the purported removal of a fundamental right, if clear words are not used, the full implication and width of the power may pass unnoticed in the democratic process (*R v Home Secretary, Ex.p Simms* [2000] 2 AC 115, 131E-F and R (*Orange Personal Communications) v Secretary of State for Trade and Industry* [2001] 3 CMLR 36 per Sullivan J at [70]).
>
> 19. Does s.124 of the Finance Act 2008 contain words of sufficient clarity to forewarn that a right of appeal from First-tier Tribunal to Upper Tribunal was to be withdrawn? There can be no dispute as to the manner in which the power may be exercised. Provisions may amend repeal or revoke any provision of any Act (S.124 (6)). But the point is not the manner in which the power may be exercised but the matter for which provision may be made.
>
> 20.The question turns on whether a provision made for revoking the right of appeal from the decision of a First-tier Tribunal to the Upper Tribunal in relation to a decision as to hardship is a 'provision . . . in connection with appeals against HMRC decisions'.
>
> 21.The paradigm of such a provision is contained within s.124 itself. S.124(2) confers power "in particular" to make provision about the circumstances in which an appeal may be made. The reference to an appeal

---

[36c] As to which, note that the number of statutory instruments, including devolved subordinate legislation, has continued to rise steeply: from 2,668 in 2002 to 4,151 in 2012.

[95a] *R. (on the application of ToTel Ltd) v First-tier Tribunal (Tax Chamber)* [2012] EWCA Civ 1401.

*

is clearly a reference to appeals under s.83 VATA 1994. The circumstances in which such appeals may be made clearly include those provisions within s.84, under the rubric 'Further provisions relating to appeals', such as the provision requiring the tax in dispute to be paid before the appeal may be entertained. Accordingly, those provisions in Paragraph 221 of the Transfer Order which omit s.84(2) and substitute s.84(3),(3A) and insert (3B) are all provisions which make provision about the circumstances in which, for example, an appeal against an assessment under s.83(p) may be made.

22. But a provision which revokes or removes a right of appeal does not seem to me properly to be described as a provision about the circumstances in which an appeal may be made. The decision of the First-tier Tribunal as to whether a taxpayer would suffer hardship if it was required to pay the tax in issue is a decision in relation to the circumstances in which an appeal may be made but is not, as is clear from the terms of s.84(3B) and its predecessor (3)(b), itself an appeal. A provision in relation to the circumstances in which an appeal may be made pre-supposes the existence of a right of appeal not its abolition."

1.3.14 [*New paragraph*]

For an example of a Henry VIII provision which is particularly extreme more in its breadth than in the substantive significance of the amendments that it permits, see the Local Government and Housing Act 1989 s.149 (statutory references to rating).

SECTION 6

CRIMINAL LEGISLATION

Distinction between criminal and civil law

1.6.3 [*New paragraph*]

In *R. (on the application of Amos) v Maidstone Crown Court*[168a] the court determined that the process of condemnation and forfeiture of goods pursuant to s.139 and Sch.3 of the Customs and Excise Management Act 1979 was civil for the purposes of art.6 of the European Convention on Human Rights.

[168a] [2013] EWCA Civ 1643.

Presumption of mental element—strict liability

[New paragraph]   **1.6.7A**

For a recent affirmation of the principle in the Supreme Court see the following passage of the single judgment in *R. v Brown (Richard)*[194a]:

> "26. The constitutional principle that mens rea is presumed to be required in order to establish criminal liability is a strong one. It is not to be displaced in the absence of clear statutory language or unmistakably necessary implication. And true it is, as the appellant has argued, that the legislative history of an enactment may not always provide the framework for deciding whether the clearly identifiable conditions in which an implication must be made are present. It is also undeniable that where the statutory offence is grave or "truly criminal" and carries a heavy penalty or a substantial social stigma, the case is enhanced against implying that mens rea of any ingredient of the offence is not needed."

[New paragraph]   **1.6.8.1**

Whatever the presumptions against and limitations on the creation of strict liability offences, there is no doubt that it is within the competence of the legislature:

> "37. We do not accept that it is the law of England and Wales that Parliament cannot provide for criminal liability when there is no causative link between the act or omission of the defendant and the prohibited event. It may be that the regulation being considered by Woodhouse J in Kilbride permitted the construction that was applied on the facts of the case before him, although the judge stated his proposition as to cause as one of legal principle. To the extent that Mr Harris seeks to derive a principle of law that even in the case of 'absolute' liability the defendant must be shown to have caused the prohibited state of affairs, we disagree with him. Such a conclusion would ignore the rationale for the acceptability of some offences of strict liability. The policy behind the prohibition may be regulatory; that is, it is in the public interest to place an absolute burden on the defendant to ensure that the state of affairs prohibited does not come about; alternatively, the criminal law may create an irrebuttable presumption whose effect cannot be avoided even by proof of moral rectitude."[201a]

[194a] [2013] UKSC 43.
[201a] *Robinson-Pierre v R* [2013] EWCA Crim 2396.

Defences placing burden on accused

1.6.13.3 *[New paragraph]*

The latest position in relation to the lawfulness of reverse burdens has been summarised and considered as follows[228a]:

"The relationship between article 6(2) of the European Convention on Human Rights and reverse onus clauses has been the subject of much consideration over the last two decades. A helpful review of the authorities on this subject was carried out by this court in *Glancy v HMA*. This review included consideration of *Salabiaku v France* (1988) 13 EHRR 379; *R v Director of Public Prosecutions ex p Kebilene* [2000] 2 A.C. 326; *R v Lambert* [2001] UKHL 37, [2002] 2 A.C. 545; *L v Director of Public Prosecutions* [2001] EWHC Admin 882, [2003] QB 137; *R v Matthews* [2003] EWCA Crim 813, [2004] QB 690, and *Sheldrake v Director of Public Prosecutions*. In light of this, we do not consider that it is necessary to repeat the passages here to which reference was made in Glancy. It is however worthwhile repeating two passages of the speech of Lord Bingham of Cornhill in *Sheldrake*, and one passage from the opinion of the court in *Glancy*, which give a clear indication of the factors which the court should have in mind when addressing the compatibility of a reverse onus clause with article 6(2).

[20] Lord Bingham of Cornhill made the following observations at paragraph 21 of his speech in *Sheldrake*:

'From this body of authority certain principles may be derived. The overriding concern is that a trial should be fair, and the presumption of innocence is a fundamental right directed to that end. The Convention does not outlaw presumptions of fact or law but requires that these should be kept within reasonable limits and should not be arbitrary. It is open to states to define the constituent elements of a criminal offence, excluding the requirement of mens rea. But the substance and effect of any presumption adverse to a defendant must be examined, and must be reasonable. Relevant to any judgment on unreasonableness or proportionality will be the opportunity given to the defendant to rebut the presumption, maintenance of the rights of the defence, flexibility in the application of the presumption, retention by the court of a power to assess the evidence, the importance of what is at stake and the difficulty which a prosecutor may face in the absence of a presumption . . .

[228a] *Derek Adam v Her Majesty's Advocate* [2013] HCJAC 14.

The justifiability of any infringement of the presumption of innocence cannot be resolved by any rule of thumb, but on examination
of all the facts and circumstances of the particular provision as
applied in the particular case.'

[21] His Lordship went on to consider the application of those principles to
section 5(2) of the Road Traffic Act 1988, and at paragraph 41 he made
the following observations:

'It may not be very profitable to debate whether section 5(2)
infringes the presumption of innocence. It may be assumed that it
does. Plainly the provision is directed to a legitimate object: the
prevention of death, injury and damage caused by unfit drivers.
Does the provision meet the tests of acceptability identified in the
Strasbourg jurisprudence? In my view, it plainly does. I do not
regard the burden placed on the defendant as beyond reasonable
limits or in any way arbitrary. It is not objectionable to criminalise
a defendant's conduct in these circumstances without requiring a
prosecutor to prove criminal intent. The defendant has a full
opportunity to show that there was no likelihood of his driving, a
matter so closely conditioned by his own knowledge and state of
mind at the material time as to make it much more appropriate for
him to prove on the balance of probabilities that he would not have
been likely to drive than for the prosecutor to prove, beyond
reasonable doubt, that he would. I do not think that imposition of a
legal burden went beyond what was necessary.'

[22] At paragraph 8 of the opinion of this court in *Glancy v HM Advocate*,
having considered *Sheldrake* and the other authorities, the court
observed that what was required was:

'a careful examination of (a) the relevant statutory provisions in
each case, (b) the measures that are taken in those provisions
directed at the activity in question, which is made an offence, and
(c) what justification can be made out for a departure from the
presumption of innocence, balancing the interests of the public and
the individual's fundamental rights.'"

Interpretation

[New paragraphs]   **1.6.16**

For considerations applied in construing and applying criminal legislation see
para.29.1.13.

1.6.17 Interaction with civil remedies

As discussed above, it can be difficult to maintain or determine the distinction between criminal and civil law. Equally, it can be difficult to determine when remedies provided, that are clearly of a non-criminal nature are intended and how they are intended, to work alongside the criminal law:

> "3. Sometimes an Act of Parliament makes it clear whether a civil remedy is available in addition to a criminal sanction. For example section 1 of the Protection from Harassment Act 1997 prohibits harassment. Section 2 creates a criminal offence; and section 3 creates a civil remedy. Conversely sections 2 to 8 of the Health and Safety at Work etc Act 1974 impose duties on employers, but section 47 (1) (a) makes it clear that there is no civil liability for breach of those duties. Sometimes, as in the Landlord and Tenant Act 1988, Parliament creates a civil remedy but imposes no criminal sanction. The problem arises where, as here, the sections in question create a criminal offence, but are silent about the availability of a civil remedy. In such cases, as the judge rightly said, the question is one of interpretation of the statute as a whole."[231a]

SECTION 8

DECLARATORY LEGISLATION

No power to make implied declaration

1.8.4.2 *[New paragraph]*

This topic is closely related to the presumption of correct law discussed in Ch.20.[312a]

SECTION 11

TAX LAW REWRITE

End of the project

1.11.9 *[New paragraph]*

The fallout from the project is still being felt: in recognition of the speed of the project powers were granted to deal by secondary legislation with the necessary consequential amendments and to make changes to restore the position in cases of unintentional change. These powers are still being exercised, as infelicities emerge from the rewritten legislation.[387a]

[231a] *Morshead Mansions Ltd v Di Marco* [2014] EWCA Civ 96.

[312a] See para.20.1.37.

[387a] See, for example, the Tax Law Rewrite Acts (Amendment) Order 2013 (SI 2013/463); the Explanatory Note to the Order says as follows: "This Order exercises the powers conferred by the Corporation Tax Act 2010 (c. 4)('CTA 2010') and the Taxation (International and Other Provisions)

Act 2010 (c. 8) ('TIOPA 2010') to make consequential amendments and undo unintended changes resulting from the work of the Tax Law Re-write project. . . . Article 10 aligns the wording used to refer to available total profits in sections 144 of CTA 2010 with that used in section 140 of that Act and in section 149(3) (as substituted by article 12 of this Order). Article 11 amends section 148 of CTA 2010 and article 12 amends section 149 of CTA 2010 to undo unintended changes to the operation of group relief from corporation tax. The changes concern limitations on what is known as consortium relief. Article 11 amends section 148 to restore the intended interaction between two restrictions on the amount eligible for surrender by a company in certain circumstances, one imposed by section 148 and the other by section 143 of CTA 2010 (known as the ownership restriction). The result is that the restriction in section 148 is applied before the restriction in section 143. Article 12 amends section 149 to undo an unintended change to the operation of two limitations on the available total profits of a company against which relief can be claimed so that the limit imposed by section 149 is applied to reduce the available total profits before that amount is further reduced by section 144 of CTA 2010."

ACTS OF PARLIAMENT

SECTION 4

IRREGULARITIES

[Add to note 70]   **2.4.4**

; see also—Gambling (Licensing and Advertising) Bill 2013–14: "The Bill engages the Technical Standards and Regulations Directive 98/34/EC (as amended by Directive 98/48/EC) and as such was required to be notified in draft to the European Commission. This has been done."

SUBORDINATE LEGISLATION

SECTION 2

COMMON FORMS OF SUBORDINATE LEGISLATION

Orders, regulations and rules

[Insert at end of paragraph "Rules are still used . . . "]   **3.2.7**

In March 2014 the UK Office of the Parliamentary Counsel published drafting guidance which includes the following change—

"Regulations, not orders

5.1.1 In Bills for the 2014-15 session and subsequent sessions, powers to make subordinate legislation by statutory instrument should generally take the form of a power to make regulations rather than an order.

5.1.2 This applies to powers to commence an Act as well as to other powers.

5.1.3 This recommendation does not alter the current practice of using—

- rules (for provision determining the procedure of a body or process),
- Orders in Council, or
- orders subject to special procedure under the Statutory Orders (Special Procedure) Act 1945.

5.1.4 There are some cases where it may still be appropriate to create a new order-making power, for example when amending an old Act that contains

13

order-making powers or when creating a new power that needs to be exercised with existing order-making powers.

5.1.5 In these transitional cases drafters should at least consider the following options—

- expressing the new power as a power to make an order;
- expressing the new power as a power to make an order or regulations;
- including a provision equivalent to section 1292 of the Companies Act 2006 (allowing provision made by order to be made by regulations and vice versa)."

3.2.9   [*Add to note 46*]

See also *R. (on the application of Alvi) v Secretary of State for the Home Department* [2012] UKSC 33; see also—"29. Although in my view it is correct to say that the views expressed by their Lordships in Odelola that the immigration rules were not statutory was not followed in *Alvi* and *Munir*, it is necessary to look more closely at both Munir and Odelola to determine whether Mr Malik's submission that the Supreme Court disapproved the premise on which the case was decided is correct or whether it supports the conclusion of Lord Dyson that the views expressed were not necessary for their decision. . . . 44. In my view a review of the full judgements in *Odelola* demonstrates that the question of whether the immigration rules are subordinate legislation was not the premise on which the case was decided." —*R. (on the application of Kumar) v Secretary of State for the Home Department* [2014] EWHC 644 (Admin); see also: "These are statements of the rules of practice which the Secretary of State and her officials follow in dealing with immigration issues. They are laid before Parliament pursuant to section 3(2) of the 1971 Act. Thus they have Parliament's tacit approval, but they are not a statutory instrument. 39. In relation to the correct approach to construing the Immigration Rules, both counsel took the court to the Supreme Court's decision in *Mahad v Entry Clearance Officer* [2009] UKSC 16; [2010] 1 W.L.R. 48. In that case the claimants were seeking to join family members settled in this country. An issue arose concerning the interpretation of rules setting out the means of support which such persons must possess. 40. Lord Brown gave the leading judgment, with which all other members of the court agreed. At paragraph 10, after referring to earlier authorities, Lord Brown stated that the Immigration Rules should not be construed with the strictness appropriate for a statute or a statutory instrument. Instead they should be construed 'sensibly according to the natural and ordinary meaning of the words used, recognising that they are statements of the Secretary of State's administrative policy'. 41. Later in the same paragraph Lord Brown said that the court could not take IDIs into account as an aid to the construction of the rules. I of course accept that proposition. There is, however, a qualification which should be noted."—*Pokhriyal v The Secretary of State for the Home Department* [2013] EWCA Civ 1568; see also— "However, as Lord Brown also said in the same paragraph in *Mahad*, the intention of the Secretary of State as embodied in the Immigration Rules has to be discerned objectively from the words used; it is not to be divined by reference to ' . . . supposed policy considerations. Still less is [that] intention to be discovered from the Immigration Directorate's Instructions ("IDIs") issued intermittently to guide immigration officers in their application of the rules'. 82. Therefore the first stop in construing the meaning of a particular Immigration Rule remains the objective construction of the words used in the Rules. If primacy is to be given to statements made after the particular rule has been laid before Parliament (pursuant to section 3(2) of the 1971 Act) and the rule has been approved by Parliament, then it would mean that the Secretary of State would be able to assert that a particular rule meant what she said it meant in a subsequent document, rather than what the rule, as approved by Parliament, stated. Such a 'Humpty Dumpty' approach to the construction of the rules would be unprincipled and entirely contrary to the rule of law and parliamentary control of the executive. In my view it is unacceptable."—*Sapkota v Secretary of State for the Home Department Court of Appeal (Civil Division)*, 15 November 2011; see also—"27.I turn therefore to Mr Drabble's principal submission, namely that on the footing that the criteria for sponsor licensing do not fall within sections 1(4) and 3(2), there is no power to have such a system at all. He submitted that this was implicit in the decisions of this court in *Munir* and *Alvi*. In particular, he relied on Lord Hope's observation in *Alvi*, at para 33, that the obligation under section 3(2) to lay statements of the rules and any changes in the rules before Parliament 'excludes the possibility of exercising prerogative powers to restrict or control immigration in ways that are not disclosed by the rules.' I do not accept that *Munir* and *Alvi* go that far. The only mode of restricting or controlling immigration which was in issue in those cases was the regulation of entry into and stay in the United Kingdom. The decisions are authority for the proposition that the power of the Secretary of State to make rules relating to the practice to be followed for regulating the entry into and stay in the United Kingdom is implicit in the obligation imposed on her by section 3(2) to lay such rules before Parliament. It has no other legal basis. Section 3(2) is concerned only with rules of that description, and it was only with the control of immigration by the grant or refusal of leave to enter or remain that Lord Hope, like the rest of the court, was concerned. The court was not concerned with the existence or extent of any power that the Secretary of State might have to do something which was not within the scope of section 3(2). 28. So in my opinion Mr. Drabble's submission is unsupported by authority. But is it right in principle? In my view it is not. It has long been recognised that the Crown possesses some general administrative powers to carry on the ordinary business of government which are not exercises of the royal prerogative and do not require statutory authority: see B.V. Harris, "The 'Third Source' of Authority for Government Action Revisited" (2007) 123 L.Q.R. 225. The extent of these powers and their exact juridical basis are controversial. In *R v Secretary of State for Health Ex p C* [2000] 1 F.L.R. 627 and *Shrewsbury and Atcham Borough Council v Secretary of State for Communities and Local Government* [2008] 3 All E.R. 548, the Court of Appeal held that the basis of the power was the Crown's status as a common law corporation sole, with all the capacities and powers of a natural person subject only to such particular limitations as were imposed by law. Although in *R (Hooper) v Secretary of State for Work and Pensions* [2005] 1 W.L.R. 1681, para 47 Lord Hoffmann thought that there was 'a good deal of force' in this analysis, it is open to question whether the analogy with a natural person is really apt in the case of public or governmental action, as opposed to purely managerial acts of a kind that any natural person could do, such as making contracts, acquiring or disposing of property, hiring and firing staff and the like. But the question does not need to be resolved on these appeals because the statutory power of the Secretary of State to administer the system of immigration control must necessarily extend to a range of ancillary and incidental administrative powers not expressly spelt out in the Act, including the vetting of sponsors. 29. The Immigration Act does not prescribe the method of immigration control to be adopted. It leaves the Secretary of State to do that, subject to her laying before Parliament any rules that she prescribes as to the practice to be followed for regulating entry into and stay in the United Kingdom. Different methods of immigration control may call for more or less elaborate administrative infrastructure. It cannot have been Parliament's intention that the Secretary of State should be limited to those methods of immigration control which required no other administrative measures apart from the regulation of entry into or stay in the United Kingdom. If the Secretary of State is entitled (as she plainly is) to prescribe and lay before Parliament rules for the grant of leave to enter or remain in the United Kingdom which depend upon the migrant having a suitable sponsor, then she must be also be entitled to take administrative measures for identifying sponsors who are and remain suitable, even if these measures do not themselves fall within section 3(2) of the Act. This right is not of course unlimited. The Secretary of State cannot adopt measures for identifying suitable sponsors which are inconsistent with the Act or the Immigration Rules. Without specific statutory authority, she cannot adopt measures which are coercive; or which infringe the legal rights of others (including their rights under the Human Rights Convention); or which are irrational or unfair or otherwise conflict with the general constraints on administrative action imposed by public law. However, she has not transgressed any of these limitations by operating a system of approved Tier 4 sponsors. It is not coercive. There are substantial advantages for sponsors in participating, but they are not obliged to do so. The rules contained in the Tier 4 Guidance for determining whether applicants are suitable to be sponsoring institutions, are in reality conditions of participation, and sponsors seeking the advantages of a licence cannot complain if they are required to adhere to them."—*R. (on the application of New London College Ltd) v Secretary of State for the Home Department* [2013] UKSC 51.

SUB-DELEGATION

[Insert at end of note 106]   **3.5.2**

For a recent and noticeably broad example of express provision in a primary enabling power allowing subordinate legislation to sub-delegate see s.31 of the Pension Schemes Act 2015: "Sub-delegation—Regulations under this Part may confer a discretion on a person."

[New paragraph]   **3.5.4**

As well as making no difference for purposes of lawfulness on whom a power to delegate is conferred, it also makes no difference how it is framed or described. A power to make regulations is obviously identifiable as a sub-delegation; however, a power to do anything that determines the ultimate effect of the law concerned is equally, although less obviously, a sub-delegation and its lawfulness or otherwise will depend on the extent of the enabling power.[111a]

SECTION 6

CHALLENGING SUBORDINATE LEGISLATION

[New paragraph]   **3.6.6.1**

The *Greenham Common* case remains one of the most important leading cases on the challenge of subordinate legislation on grounds of being ultra vires, and it is frequently relied upon expressly by the courts. For a recent example reprising the case's key principles and their application see *R. (on the application of T) v Chief Constable of Greater Manchester*[128a]—

"57. When is subordinate legislation ultra vires? A leading, relatively recent, example is *Director of Public Prosecutions v Hutchinson* [1990] 2 A.C. 783. The Secretary of State for Defence made a byelaw prohibiting all

---

[111a] See, for example: "It is said that, by merely providing that the Secretary of State may select a claimant for participation in a scheme, it suffers from the same vice as the alleged prescribed description of the schemes, in that it does no more than sub-delegate, in a completely unqualified way, the whole exercise of prescribing the circumstances to the Secretary of State. However, as Pill LJ indicated in para.58 of his judgment, one must also consider regulation 4 in this context. It seems to us that, particularly given the need for flexibility, regulation 4 contains sufficient detail to justify the conclusion that the circumstances in which a claimant can be required to participate in a scheme is to be 'determined in accordance with' the 2011 Regulations. The fact that the regulation is concerned with the contents of a notice is irrelevant to this issue, but the very open-ended nature of what is left to the Secretary of State by regulation 4 could well be a problem in other circumstances where flexibility was not so obviously essential."—*R. (on the application of Reilly) v Secretary of State for Work and Pensions* [2013] UKSC 68.

[128a] [2014] UKSC 35.

entry into designated land at Greenham Common without authority. His statutory authority for doing so was expressed not to extend to interference with any right of common. It turned out that there were 62 commoners who had rights to take gravel and wood from, and to graze animals on, part of the land which he had designated. So he had no power to prohibit entry in such unqualified terms. Then the question arose whether the byelaw could be severed so that its validity could be retained in respect of people who, like the appellants, were not commoners yet had entered the land. To this the House of Lords gave a negative answer. It held, at p 811, that the fact that the invalid feature of the byelaw could not be excised with a blue pen did not preclude severance. What precluded it was that, if the byelaw was so construed as to allow the 62 commoners to enter the land, the legislative purpose behind it would be undermined: p 813. By way of contrast the House cited with approval *Dunkley v Evans* [1981] 1 W.L.R. 1522, in which the Minister of Agriculture had made an order prohibiting fishing for herring in designated waters. One per cent of the area which he designated was a stretch of water off Northern Ireland which he had no power to include in his designation. The respondents had been fishing for herring in the remaining 99% of the area. The Divisional Court held that the order was severable and that the respondents should have been convicted. These then, are examples of the classic situation in which the width of the subordinate legislation exceeds the contours expressed in the authority for it to be made. 58. Sometimes the court decides that the operation of a piece of subordinate legislation has violated fundamental rights in circumstances in which the logic of the decision means that its operation will always violate fundamental rights. A good example is *A v HM Treasury* [2010] UKSC 2, [2010] 2 A.C. 534. By a subparagraph of an article of an order purportedly made pursuant to the United Nations Act 1946, the Treasury provided that any person listed by the Sanctions Committee of the United Nations, on the basis that he was associated with an organisation threatening international peace, was a designated person for the purposes of another order, which dramatically deprived him of access to financial resources. Two of the parties before the court had been so listed. The Supreme Court held that the absence in the order of a facility for them to mount a domestic challenge to the basis of their listing by the Sanctions Committee ran counter to their fundamental rights. The court therefore held that the subparagraph was ultra vires but that a judge had been wrong to declare the whole order to be ultra vires: paras 81 and 83 (Lord Hope) and para 241 (Lord Mance). It is easy to see that the vice of the order was not related to the particular circumstances of the two parties who had been listed: the rights of every person listed by the Sanctions Committee would be violated by the absence in the order of a facility for challenge."—*R. (on the application of T) v Chief Constable of Greater Manchester* [2014] UKSC 35.

SECTION 7

RARER FORMS OF SUBORDINATE LEGISLATION AND QUASI-LEGISLATION

Introduction to "soft law"

[New paragraph]   **3.7.A1**

Different forms of quasi-legislation are assuming increasing importance all the time. Only a few years ago, legislation was clearly divided into primary legislation and secondary legislation, and apart from a few codes of conduct and the admittedly exceptional Immigration Rules, almost all legislation was drafted in a straightforwardly "hard letter" form. Nowadays, scarcely a single Act of Parliament is passed without conferring a range of powers to issue schemes, codes, guidance, directions and other forms of instrument all of which, classify them as legislation or quasi-legislation as you will, in one sense or another, and to one extent or another, change the law.

Most of these miscellaneous instruments are drafted in a "soft law" form, meaning that instead of conferring and imposing clear and justiciable rights and duties, they set open principles which are to have some kind of effect in relation to rights or duties set by other hard-letter legislation.

Soft-law quasi-legislation undoubtedly has great uses, and is able to achieve changes with a finesse that is beyond the reach of hard-law primary or secondary legislation. But this flexibility inevitably involves a lack of clarity, in the sense of denying the reader the ability to know clearly what is and is not required or promised.

Later passages of this Section describe aspects of particular kinds of quasi-legislation.

The essence of the citizens' expectations of quasi-legislation generally is discussed in *AAM (A Child) v Secretary of State for the Home Department*[136a]:

> "In considering the meaning of the Defendant's policy, I have had regard to the guidance given in *R (Anam) v Secretary of State for the Home Department* [2009] EWHC 2496 (Admin). Cranston J. confirmed that it was for the court to decide the meaning of a policy objectively. He said, at [49]:
>
>> '49. The meaning of a policy such as that contained in the Enforcement Instructions and Guidance is an objective matter: *R (on the application of Raissi) v Secretary of State for the Home Department* [2008] EWCA Civ 72. In that case the Court of Appeal considered how such schemes should be interpreted and referred to Lord Steyn's speech in *In Re McFarland* [2005] UKHL 17; [2004] 1 W.L.R. 1289. Lord Steyn's speech also goes

---

[136a] [2012] EWHC 2567 (QB).

to the point that persons are entitled to rely on the language of a policy statement.

"[24] . . . In my view, however, in respect of the many kinds of "soft laws" with which we are now familiar, one must bear in mind that citizens are led to believe that the carefully drafted and considered statements truly represent government policy which will be observed in decision-making unless there is good reason to depart from it. It is an integral part of the working of a mature process of public administration. Such policy statements are an important source of individual rights and corresponding duties. In a fair and effective public law system such policy statements must be interpreted objectively in accordance with the language employed by the Minister. The citizen is entitled to rely on the language of the statement, seen as always in its proper context. The very reason for making the statement is to give guidance to the public. The decision-maker, here a Minister, may depart from the policy but until he has done so, the citizen is entitled to ask in a court of law whether he fairly comes within the language of the publicly announced policy."

50. . . . The upshot in Raissi was that the Court of Appeal decided that the meaning of a policy was a 'hard-edged question' which fell to be determined objectively by the courts and not by the minister responsible for administering the scheme.'"

Codes of practice

Non-statutory codes

3.7.3.1.1 *[New paragraph]*

The approach of the courts to non-statutory codes and the weight to be attached to them are discussed as follows in *Devon CC v TR*[149a] in the following words:

"Despite the recognition in the opening words that the code was non-mandatory, this approach amounted to treating it as a mandatory standard which had to be adhered to unless there was a positive reason to depart from it. Whilst the code is clearly evidence of general good practice, its status must not be overstated. It has no statutory basis and its own terms are explicit in a section carefully entitled 'Status of the Code' (this quotation is taken from the 2005 Code; the 2001 Code contains an almost exactly similar passage):

[149a] [2013] EWCA Civ 418.

'1.3.1 The suggested recommendations of this Code are explicitly not mandatory on authorities. The key best value principle of requiring authorities to involve users in the design and delivery of service implies that authorities should have reasonable discretion to respond to such involvement.

1.3.2 Authorities also have certain legal obligations with which they need to comply, and which will, on occasion, be the subject of claims or legal action. . . . It has been recognised that in such cases the contents of this Code may be considered to be a relevant consideration. In these circumstances, where authorities elect, in the light of local circumstances to adopt policies, procedures or standards differing from those suggested by the Code it is essential for these to be identified, together with the reasoning for such differences.'

The key statement is that at the outset. The code does not set out mandatory rules. It is evidence of good practice. Authorities must exercise their own judgment. The second sentence of 1.3.1 is clearly simply an example of the kind of consideration which might be relevant. When it comes to the specific issue of inspection intervals, other considerations will clearly include traffic use, experience, the frequency of adverse incidents and the like. The advice in 1.3.2, to make explicit reasons for adopting different policies is clearly wise, given the exposure of highway authorities to the possibility of litigation. But it is advice, not a rule. It cannot amount to a rule that it will of itself be a want of reasonable care to adopt a different inspection interval unless some particular process of reasoning is passed through, and set out somewhere in writing; if it did, that also would be to make the code a mandatory instrument. The judge's approach amounted to treating paragraph 1.3.2 as a mandatory rule of procedure, justifying a procedural and/or reasons challenge if it were not complied with, and then the inspection interval as a prescribed rule in the absence of demonstrated reasons for departure."

Guidance

[Insert at end of note 160] **3.7.4.2**

; see also, "However, as Lord Brown also said in the same paragraph in *Mahad*, the intention of the Secretary of State as embodied in the Immigration Rules has to be discerned objectively from the words used; it is not to be divined by reference to ' . . . supposed policy considerations. Still less is [that] intention to be discovered from the Immigration Directorate's Instructions ("IDIs") issued intermittently to guide immigration officers in their application of the rules'. 82. Therefore the first stop in construing the meaning of a particular Immigration Rule remains the objective construction of the words used in the Rules. If primacy is to be given to statements made after the particular rule has been laid before Parliament (pursuant to section 3(2) of the 1971 Act) and the rule has been approved by Parliament, then it would mean that the Secretary of State would be able to assert that a particular rule meant what she said it meant in a subsequent document, rather than what the rule, as approved by Parliament, stated. Such a "Humpty Dumpty" approach to the construction of the rules would be unprincipled and entirely contrary to the rule of law and parliamentary control of the executive. In my view it is unacceptable."—*Sapkota v Secretary of State for the Home Department Court of Appeal (Civil Division)*, November 15, 2011.

Statutory guidance

3.7.4.3 [*New paragraph*]

Judicial discussion of the weight to be given to statutory guidance is found in *R. (on the application of X) v Tower Hamlets LBC*[161a] in the following words:

> "35. In summary, therefore, the guidance does not have the binding effect of secondary legislation and a local authority is free to depart from it, even 'substantially'. But a departure from the guidance will be unlawful unless there is a cogent reason for it, and the greater the departure, the more compelling must that reason be. Conversely a minor departure from the letter of the guidance while remaining true to its spirit may well be easy to justify or may not even be regarded as a departure at all. The court will scrutinise carefully the reason given by the authority for departing from the guidance. Freedom to depart is not necessarily limited to reasons resulting from 'local circumstances' (see [18] above), although if there are particular local circumstances which suggest that some aspect of the guidance ought not to apply, that may constitute a cogent reason for departure. However, except perhaps in the case of a minor departure, it is difficult to envisage circumstances in which mere disagreement with the guidance could amount to a cogent reason for departing from it."

There are strict limits on the force which can be given to Guidance issued by Ministers. In the case of statutory Guidance, the extent of its effect must be clearly stipulated by the enabling legislation. In the case of non-statutory Guidance, it has no authority either to legislate or to determine the meaning or application of legislation. Despite that, however, readers including judges

---

[161a] [2013] EWHC 480 (Admin).

may be tempted to invest Guidance with a degree of authority simply because of its apparent form and official provenance.[161b]

[New paragraph] **3.7.4.4**

In theory there is nothing to prevent a Department or other recipient of a power to give guidance to draft it in a hard-letter form that appears to set clear justiciable rules, whether the statutory requirement is to comply with or merely to have regard to the guidance. The courts will, however, give form precedence over substance to the extent of inferring that a statutory decision to confer a power to give guidance deliberately falls short of a power to make the kind of inflexible rules that are appropriate for secondary legislation.[161c]

Church Measures

[New paragraph] **3.7.7.1**

An illuminating correspondence between the Legal Adviser to the Archbishop's Council and the Clerk to the House of Lords Select Committee on the Merits of Statutory Instruments, as printed in a Report of the Committee is set out in the Appendix as Extract 8AA.

Royal Charter

[New paragraph] **3.7.8.1**

Statute may also operate by reference to a body created by Charter or may expressly preserve the effect of a provision of a Charter. A particularly significant recent example arose in connection with the issue of press-regulation following the Leveson report. In the course of this process, the

---

[161b] See, for example: "32. I had doubts as to whether suspending an officer merely in order to prevent him resigning was a proper exercise of the power under reg. 4, when there was no perceived need to remove him from active deployment, which on a literal reading of reg. 4, is its purpose. However, in the light of the guidance from the Secretary of State, I conclude that reg. 4 was intended to have a wider purpose and so the Defendant was entitled to exercise the reg. 4 power to prevent the Claimant resigning, on public interest grounds. I accept the Defendant's submission that the terms of reg. 4(1) confer a broad discretion on the appropriate authority. However, that discretion is subject to the conditions in reg. 4(2). An officer can only be suspended in the public interest if this course is"require". I agree with Stuart-Smith J. that this "carries the implication that the public interest leaves no other course open" (see *R (Rhodes) v Police and Crime Commissioner for Lincolnshire* [2013] EWHC 1009 (Admin))."—*R. (on the application of Birks) v Commissioner of Police of the Metropolis* [2014] EWHC 3041 (Admin).

[161c] "It seems to me that, as a matter of ordinary language, there is a clear distinction between guidance and a rule. Guidance is advisory in character; it assists the decision maker but does not compel a particular outcome. By contrast a rule is mandatory in nature; it compels the decision maker to reach a particular result."—*R. (on the application of Alvi) v Secretary of State for the Home Department* [2012] UKSC 33.

Government refused to provide for a statutory corporation regulating the press, but in effect struck a compromise between statutory regulation and self-regulation by giving statutory recognition in a number of places to a body established by Charter: see, in particular, the Crime and Courts Act 2013 s.42 (Publishers of news-related material: damages and costs: Other interpretative provisions—"Approved regulator" means a body recognised as a regulator of relevant publishers. (3) For the purposes of subsection (2), a body is "recognised" as a regulator of relevant publishers if it is so recognised by any body established by Royal Charter (whether established before or after the coming into force of this section) with the purpose of carrying on activities relating to the recognition of independent regulators of relevant publishers.").

The status and implications of Charters as a quasi-legislative instrument came under close scrutiny in the case of *R. (on the application of Project Management Institute) v Minister for the Cabinet Office Queen's Bench Division*[176a]—

"2. This is, I believe, the first time that the grant or refusal of a Royal Charter has been the subject of litigation. I propose, therefore, to begin by a brief analysis of the history and nature of Royal Charters and the process by which they are granted. A Royal Charter is granted in the exercise of prerogative powers 'the residue of discretionary or arbitrary authority, which at any given time is legally left in the hands of the Crown': Dicey, *The Law of the Constitution* p424. It has the essential qualities of an executive, rather than legislative, act and is 'best not described as legislation': *Craies on Legislation* 10th Edition paragraph 3.7.8. Its original purpose was to grant corporate personality to bodies of persons conducting activities for public or private benefit. The first Royal Charter in the first category was granted to the University of Cambridge in 1231 and in the second to the Sadlers Company in 1272. Numerous grants have been made to educational institutions and livery companies ever since. The first grant of a Royal Charter to a group of persons carrying on a profession was to the Royal College of Physicians of London in 1518. At the turn of the 17th and 18th centuries, Royal Charters were granted to institutions which played a major part in the economic life of the country, notably the Bank of England in 1694 and the South Sea Company in 1711. The puncturing of the South Sea bubble in 1720 caused Parliament to prohibit the formation of joint stock companies except by Royal Charter in the Bubble Act 1720. Thereafter until

---

[176a] *R. (on the application of Project Management Institute) v Minister for the Cabinet Office Queen's Bench Division (Administrative Court)* July 17, 2014 [2014] EWHC 2438 (Admin).

the early 19th century, the grant of Royal Charters in the economic field was limited to a small number of banks and insurance companies. Between the enactment of the Chartered Companies Act 1837 and the Limited Liability Act 1855, the grant of a Royal Charter was the principal means by which economic activity could be carried on by an incorporated body without putting at risk the entire assets of those who subscribed capital to it. In consequence, a large number of trading and mining companies were incorporated by Royal Charter between those dates. Few were afterwards. From then on, the great majority of bodies incorporated by Royal Charter have been educational, charitable or professional. Lord Diplock was not quite right when he identified this function of the Privy Council as "the grant of corporate personality to deserving bodies of persons" in *Council of Civil Service Unions v Minister for the Civil Service* [1985] A.C. 374 at 410B, because almost all of the grantees have already been incorporated under legislative provisions. Grants are still made to unincorporated groups of persons for example livery companies and, in 2012, Marylebone Cricket Club—but current practice is accurately stated by the Privy Council on its website: 'New grants of Royal Charters are these days reserved for eminent professional bodies or charities which have a solid record of achievement and are financially sound'.

3. An organisation seeking the grant of a Royal Charter must petition Her Majesty the Queen in Council. On its website, the Privy Council Office invites informal approaches before a petition is lodged, to afford that office the opportunity of giving advice about the chances of success. Petitioners are advised to take soundings amongst other bodies which may have an interest in the outcome. Once a formal petition has been lodged, it is advertised in the London Gazette. Any objector is entitled within six weeks to lodge a counter-petition. The petition is considered by a sub-committee of the Privy Council, comprising Ministers of the departments most closely connected with the activities of the petitioner. Unanimity amongst the members of the committee is required before a recommendation for the grant of a Royal Charter will be made.

4. A petitioner is required to submit a draft of its Charter and by-laws. Both must be approved by the Attorney General. Once a Royal Charter is granted, the Charter and by-laws cannot be amended without the consent of the Privy Council. I am led to understand by Miss Steyn QC, counsel for the defendants, that the Privy Council's oversight of Chartered bodies is ordinarily reactive, but it does retain the power to recommend revocation of a Charter, last exercised in 1684 in respect of the Somers Isles Company, and is prepared to threaten the use of the power in appropriate circumstances. She told me that there had been one such occurrence in recent times."

Foreign legislation

3.7.19.1 *[New paragraph]*

For the principles to be applied in construing foreign legislation for the purposes of the UK courts, see the following:

"8. The principles to be applied when an English court has to decide the effect of a foreign statute are well established and have not been the subject of any dispute. In particular:

a) Matters of foreign law are treated in an English court as matters of fact which must generally be proved by expert evidence.

b) Where the relevant foreign law is contained in a code or other legislation, the relevant question is how a court in the foreign jurisdiction would interpret the legislation.

c) The primary evidence to be used in answering that question is evidence of the opinions of expert witnesses. As with any expert evidence, however, the court is entitled and may be bound to look at the sources on which the experts rely in order to decide what weight to give to their opinions."[219a]

SECTION 10

INSTRUMENTS IMPLEMENTING COMMUNITY OBLIGATIONS

3.10.3 *[Insert at end of note 322]*

; see also—"Regulation 13(1) cannot be read down in the way he suggested. That this was the intention is made clear in the Explanatory Memorandum to the Regulations, para 3.5. Applying EU instruments in this way is possible under the regulation-making power in section 2(2) of the European Communities Act 1972, which empowers the making of regulations not only to implement an EU obligation but for the purpose of "dealing with matters arising out of or related to any such obligation or rights": see *Oakley Inc v Animal Ltd* [2006] Ch 337, [20]–[33]."—*R. (on the application of Lumsdon) v Legal Services Board* [2014] EWHC 28 (Admin).

The "copy-out" debate

3.10.3.1 *[Insert at end of note 325]*

; see also—"32. I fully accept that not every 'relationship' between a Community obligation and a provision made by secondary legislation will satisfy the

---

[219a] *Iraqi Civilian Litigation v Ministry of Defence* [2015] EWHC 116 (QB).

requirements of section 2 (2) (b). It is clear from the judgments in *Oakley v Animal* that it is necessary in any given case to consider whether the provision in question is of a kind which Parliament must have intended to be capable of being enacted by secondary legislation: see in particular the judgments of Waller LJ at para. 39 (p. 352) and May LJ at para. 47 (p. 353)[4]. But I think it is plain that that is the case here. The decision to go beyond the requirements of the Directive by extending the 'employee representative' rights to employees in PABs (except those in Crown employment) may, as a matter of strict analysis, reflect a substantive policy choice made by the Secretary of State; but, as the judgments in *Oakley* make clear, that is not in itself objectionable. In fact all that he was doing was plugging the rights created by the Regulations in cases where no trade union was recognised into the pre-existing scheme of the Act and thereby reproducing, in the case of this late-discovered lacuna in the implementation of the Directive, the selfsame decision as Parliament had already made in enacting the primary legislation in 1975 and 1992. It would indeed have been an extraordinary anomaly if the kinds of employment where the obligation to consult arose differed as between cases where a trade union was recognised and cases where it was not; and it was not only natural but right for the Secretary of State in making the Regulations to ensure that the position was the same in both cases. In my judgment this is precisely the kind of 'closely related original choice which the Directive does not . . . require' but which 'has the effect of tidying things up' that May LJ identifies in his judgment in *Animal v Oakley* (loc. cit-.)."—*The United States of America v Nolan* [2014] EWCA Civ 71.

[Add after note 344]   **3.10.8.1**

There are signs that the technique of disregarding the implementing domestic legislation and construing the European Union legislation directly is gaining traction.[344a]

SECTION 12

TRANSFER OF FUNCTIONS ORDERS

Joint exercise versus concurrent exercise

[Add new note 386a after "Where a function is vested in two Ministers   **3.12.6**
concurrently, either may perform it, acting alone, on any occasion."]

[344a] See, for example, "13. The relevant EU legislation is contained in Council Directive 67/227/EEC of 11 April 1967 on the harmonisation of legislation of Member States concerning turnover taxes ('the First Directive'), and the Sixth Directive, as amended by Council Directive 95/7/EC of 10 April 1995. These are translated into domestic law by the Value Added Tax Act 1994. It is sufficient to refer to the EU provisions."—*Revenue and Customs v Aimia Coalition Loyalty UK Ltd* [2013] UKSC 15.

Note that this proposition has received judicial approval in the following terms: "Thirdly, *Craies on Legislation* 10th ed, (2012) supports the notion that the concept of concurrent power to exercise functions has an established meaning in legislation. At para 3.12.6, it is stated that '[w]here a function is vested in two Ministers concurrently, either may perform it, acting alone, on any occasion'. While no case law is cited in support of this proposition, such an unequivocal statement in a respected book on the subject deserves respect, and is likely to be familiar to those responsible for drafting statutes."—Local Government Byelaws (Wales) Bill 2012. Reference by the Attorney General for England and Wales [2012] UKSC 53.

CHAPTER 4

DEVOLVED LEGISLATION

SECTION 4

WALES

[Replaces the existing text in Section 4]

Introduction

The Government of Wales Act 1998[129] first gave effect to the policy of Welsh **4.4.1** devolution. The principal difference between that and the 1998 devolution Acts for Scotland and Northern Ireland was that the Assembly had no power to initiate legislation of a character akin to primary legislation. The Government of Wales Act 2006[130] changed that, introducing powers for the National Assembly for Wales very much like those of the Scottish Parliament or the Northern Ireland Assembly.

Unlike the devolution of power to Scotland and Northern Ireland, however, even under the 2006 Act the power to make devolved legislation was granted in two stages. During the Third Assembly, there was a power to make Measures under Pt 3 of the Act. The power to pass Acts of the Assembly was contained in Pt 4 of the 2006 Act and was contingent on the passing of a referendum[131] approving the commencement of that power. The majority of voters in a referendum had to vote for the Assembly Act provisions to come into force, following which there was a duty to bring them into force by commencement order made by the Welsh Ministers. By virtue of s.106 of the 2006 Act, once the Assembly Act provisions came into force, Pt 3 of the Act ceased to have effect and the Assembly no longer has the power to pass Measures. Anything that would previously have been achieved by Measure can and must now be achieved

---

[129] 1998 c.38.
[130] 2006 c.32.
[131] Under s.103.

by Act of the Assembly. Measures already enacted, however, continue to be law; so although none has been passed since the beginning of the Fourth Assembly, many remain in force and are likely to be of practical importance for a considerable length of time.

Acts of the National Assembly

4.4.2 Section 107 of the Government of Wales Act 2006 allows the National Assembly for Wales to make laws:

> **"107 Acts of the Assembly**
>
> (1) The Assembly may make laws, to be known as Acts of the National Assembly for Wales or Deddfau Cynulliad Cenedlaethol Cymru (referred to in this Act as "Acts of the Assembly").
> (2) Proposed Acts of the Assembly are to be known as Bills; and a Bill becomes an Act of the Assembly when it has been passed by the Assembly and has received Royal Assent.
> (3) The validity of an Act of the Assembly is not affected by any invalidity in the Assembly proceedings leading to its enactment.
> (4) Every Act of the Assembly is to be judicially noticed.
> (5) This Part does not affect the power of the Parliament of the United Kingdom to make laws for Wales."

Use made of the power

4.4.3 Two Acts were passed in 2012; seven in 2013; seven in 2014; and when this supplement went to press, three Acts had been passed in 2015.[131]

Legislative competence

4.4.4 As in the case of devolution in Northern Ireland and Scotland, the potential scope of Acts of the National Assembly is determined by the concept of legislative competence.

There is, however, a fundamental difference in relation to devolution in Wales: the Scottish Parliament and Northern Ireland Assembly are assumed to have

---

[131] Well-being of Future Generations (Wales) Act 2015; Violence against Women, Domestic Abuse and Sexual Violence (Wales) Act 2015; Higher Education (Wales) Act 2015; Housing (Wales) Act 2014; Agricultural Sector (Wales) Act 2014; Education (Wales) Act 2014; Social Services and Well-being (Wales) Act 2014; Control of Horses (Wales) Act 2014; National Health Service Finance (Wales) Act 2014; Further and Higher Education (Governance and Information) (Wales) Act 2014; Active Travel (Wales) Act 2013; Mobile Homes (Wales) Act 2013; Human Transplantation (Wales) Act 2013; Local Government (Democracy) (Wales) Act 2013; Public Audit (Wales) Act 2013; Food Hygiene Rating (Wales) Act 2013; School Standards and Organisation (Wales) Act 2013; Local Government Byelaws (Wales) Act 2012; and National Assembly for Wales (Official Languages) Act 2012.

competence unless the proposed Bill falls within one of the exceptions to their competence. By contrast, the National Assembly for Wales does not have competence unless it falls within one of the designated areas.

Section 108 of the 2006 Act provides as follows:

"(1) Subject to the provisions of this Part, an Act of the Assembly may make any provision that could be made by an Act of Parliament.[132]

(2) An Act of the Assembly is not law so far as any provision of the Act is outside the Assembly's legislative competence.

(3) A provision of an Act of the Assembly is within the Assembly's legislative competence only if it falls within subsection (4) or (5).

(4) A provision of an Act of the Assembly falls within this subsection if—

(a) it relates to one or more of the subjects listed under any of the headings in Part 1 of Schedule 7 and does not fall within any of the exceptions specified in that Part of that Schedule (whether or not under that heading or any of those headings), and

(b) it neither applies otherwise than in relation to Wales nor confers, imposes, modifies or removes (or gives power to confer, impose, modify or remove) functions exercisable otherwise than in relation to Wales.

(5) A provision of an Act of the Assembly falls within this subsection if—

(a) it provides for the enforcement of a provision (of that or any other Act of the Assembly) which falls within subsection (4) or a provision of an Assembly Measure or it is otherwise appropriate for making such a provision effective, or

(b) it is otherwise incidental to, or consequential on, such a provision.

(6) But a provision which falls within subsection (4) or (5) is outside the Assembly's legislative competence if—

(a) it breaches any of the restrictions in Part 2 of Schedule 7, having regard to any exception in Part 3 of that Schedule from those restrictions,

(b) it extends otherwise than only to England and Wales, or

(c) it is incompatible with the Convention rights or with EU law.

---

[132] This proposition is not about the areas in which the Assembly is entitled to operate, but about the kind of provision that may be made within the areas of competence; so, for example, unlike secondary legislation which is subject to a presumption against sub-delegation, it will be presumed that it is open to an Act of the Assembly to further delegate legislative power, but only within the permitted areas of competence.

(7) For the purposes of this section the question whether a provision of an Act of the Assembly relates to one or more of the subjects listed in Part 1 of Schedule 7 (or falls within any of the exceptions specified in that Part of that Schedule) is to be determined by reference to the purpose of the provision, having regard (among other things) to its effect in all the circumstances."

4.4.5   It is therefore Sch.7 that from time to time sets out the definite list of topics which an Act of the National Assembly may deal with. The latest text[133] of Sch.7 is set out in Annex C to this supplement.

When a Bill is introduced in the Assembly, the person in charge of it must state that in their view its provisions would be within the Assembly's legislative competence.[134] The Presiding Officer must also state whether or not it is within the areas of competence.[135]

Challenges to competence—general

4.4.6   The Counsel General or the Attorney General may refer the question of whether a provision of a Bill would be within the legislative competence of the Assembly to the Supreme Court.[136] A reference must be made within four weeks of the passing or approval after reconsideration of the Bill.[137]

Since the competence of the National Assembly for Wales is entirely statutory, the methods of challenge are also explicit in statute. In essence, the Government of Wales Act 2006 provides express procedures through which the legislative competence of an Act of the National Assembly for Wales can be challenged. Importantly, however, since legislative competence is a condition of validity, apart from the express statutory procedures it is always open to anyone affected by an Act of the National Assembly to challenge its validity on grounds of lack of legislative competence.

The Government of Wales Act 2006 s.108(2) provides that: "An Act of the Assembly is not law so far as any provision of the Act is outside the Assembly's legislative competence."

4.4.7   Within the Assembly's legislative competence "an Act of the Assembly may make any provision that could be made by an Act of Parliament": s.108(1). That means the Assembly has the same breadth of powers as Parliament when

---

[133] There is power to amend the Schedule by Order in Council under s.109; see the National Assembly for Wales (Legislative Competence) (Amendment of Schedule 7 to the Government of Wales Act 2006) Order 2007 (SI 2007/2143) and the National Assembly for Wales (Legislative Competence) (Amendment of Schedule 7 to the Government of Wales Act 2006) Order 2010 (SI 2010/2968).

[134] 2006 Act s.110(2).

[135] 2006 Act s.110(3).

[136] 2006 Act s.112.

[137] s.112(2).

legislating: the Government's Explanatory Notes say (in relation to the Measures, which Assembly Acts replaced) that: "In other words it can, for example, modify existing Acts of Parliament or other enactments and it can make new provision not covered by existing statutes."

Section 108(1) does not, however, give the Assembly the same breadth of privileges and immunities as Parliament. In particular, once an Act of Parliament is passed the courts will not inquire into the propriety of the proceedings that led up to Royal Assent: but the same deference is not to be shown to the National Assembly. Section 107(3) of the 2006 Act provides that "The validity of an Act of the Assembly is not affected by any invalidity in the Assembly proceedings leading to its enactment"; but that falls short of the kind of immunity from consideration by the courts that art.9 of the Bill of Rights provides for Acts of Parliament; in particular, it allows for circumvention along *Anisminic* lines, and as the Government's Explanatory Notes to the Act acknowledge "it is thought that this subsection will not save a purported Act which had not been passed by the Assembly at all because, in those circumstances, section 107(2) would not have been complied with".

Competence—Attorney General's challenge

Section 112(1) of the 2006 Act provides that: **4.4.8**

> " . . . the Attorney General may refer the question whether a Bill, or any provision of a Bill, would be within the Assembly's legislative competence to the Supreme Court for decision."

In order to provide a degree of legal certainty (but see the reference below to perpetual challenge), references under s.112(1) must be made "at any time during—(a) the period of four weeks beginning with the passing of the Bill, and (b) any period of four weeks beginning with any subsequent approval of the Bill in accordance with provision included in the standing orders in compliance with s.111(7)".[138]

Under s.112(3) "no reference may be made in relation to a Bill . . . by the Attorney General if the Attorney General has notified the Clerk that no reference is to be made in relation to it by the Attorney General". This is again designed to give a degree of legal certainty, and is subject to the same exception for Bills approved in compliance with s.111(7).

---

[138] Section 111(7) provides that "The standing orders must, in particular, ensure that any Bill amended on reconsideration is subject to a final stage at which it can be approved or rejected".

4.4.9   The Attorney General challenged the first Act passed by the National Assembly.[139] The challenge was completely unsuccessful. Although Lord Neuberger's judgment is at pains to suggest that the case does not set a precedent, the Supreme Court made a number of observations that are clearly deliberately general in their potential application. An extract from Lord Neuberger's judgment appears at Annex D to this supplement.

The Attorney General referred the Agricultural Sector (Wales) Bill, passed by the National Assembly, to the Supreme Court; the Attorney's letter to the National Assembly of August 9, 2013 expressed the hope that the reference will bring clarity in relation to "important questions about the breadth of the National Assembly's competence". The reference was decided as *Attorney General for England and Wales v Counsel General for Wales* [2014] UKSC 43; [2014] 1 W.L.R. 2622. The Bill established a scheme for the regulation of agricultural wages in Wales. Until 2013, the Agricultural Wages Act 1948 provided a regime for regulating agricultural wages for England and Wales under an Agricultural Advisory Panel for Wales, which was abolished by the UK Parliament under the Enterprise and Regulatory Reform Act 2013. The Welsh Government wished to retain a regime for the regulation of agricultural wages in Wales, hence the Bill. The Assembly relied on its competence to make legislation which "relates to . . . Agriculture. Horticulture. Forestry. Fisheries and fishing. Animal Health and welfare. Plant health. Plant varieties and seeds. Rural development". The UK Government argued that the Bill was really about the non-devolved area of employment and industrial relations. The court found the Bill within competence, partly by reference to the legislative background to the regulation of agricultural wages in the UK and partly as a matter of following the statutory development of devolution to Wales in three legislative phases.

As well as Attorney General's references, the Counsel General (appointed by the Welsh Government) can refer a Bill to the Supreme Court for a decision on competence, as discussed below.Thepower has been exercised: *Reference by the Counsel General for Wales, Recovery of Medical Costs for Asbestos Diseases (Wales) Bill, Re* [2015] UKSC 3; [2015] 2 W.L.R. 481: in that case the Supreme Court found that the Welsh Assembly lacked legislative competence to enact the Recovery of Medical Costs for Asbestos Diseases (Wales) Bill on the grounds that it was outside the legislative competence category of the "organisation and funding of [the] national health service" and that it was incompatible with the rights of compensators and insurers to the peaceful enjoyment of their possessions under the European Convention on Human Rights.

Competence—Counsel General's Challenge

4.4.10   Section 112(1) of the 2006 Act provides that "the Counsel General may refer the question whether a Bill, or any provision of a Bill, would be within the Assembly's legislative competence to the Supreme Court for decision".

---

[139] *Attorney General v National Assembly for Wales Commission* [2012] UKSC 53.

In order to provide a degree of legal certainty (but see the reference below to perpetual challenge), references under s.112(1) must be made "at any time during—(a) the period of four weeks beginning with the passing of the Bill, and (b) any period of four weeks beginning with any subsequent approval of the Bill in accordance with provision included in the standing orders in compliance with s.111(7)". (Section 111(7) provides that "The standing orders must, in particular, ensure that any Bill amended on reconsideration is subject to a final stage at which it can be approved or rejected").

Under s.112(3), "no reference may be made in relation to a Bill . . . by the Counsel General if the Counsel General has notified the Clerk that no reference is to be made in relation to it by the Counsel General". This is again designed to give a degree of legal certainty, and is subject to the same exception for Bills approved in compliance with s.111(7).

The most obvious reason why the Counsel General might wish to refer a Bill **4.4.11** to the Supreme Court is so as to provide a quick end to uncertainty by pre-empting other forms of possible challenge, inviting a clear decision from the Supreme Court that the Bill is within legislative competence.

It is also, however, possible to imagine the power being exercised by the Counsel General where the Welsh Government are of the opinion that a Bill, or a provision of a Bill, passed by the Assembly contrary to the Welsh Government's policy and advice, is unlawful on the grounds of lack of competence.

Challenge to competence—European Court of Justice Involvement

One of the grounds on which legislative competence is limited is the proposition **4.4.12** that "a provision which falls within subsection (4) or (5) is outside the Assembly's legislative competence if it is incompatible with the Convention rights or with EU law": s.108(6).

As a result, it is possible that a challenge to an Assembly Act taken to the Supreme Court on the grounds of non-compliance with EU law may have to be referred by the Supreme Court to the European Court of Justice, so as to obtain an authoritative ruling on the meaning of the relevant EU law (see the European Communities Act 1972 s.3).

Where a challenge has been referred by the Supreme Court to the ECJ, the Assembly can decide to reconsider the Bill, in which case the reference is stayed under s.113 of the 2006 Act.

Secretary of State control

Section 114 of the 2006 Act gives the Secretary of State power to control certain **4.4.13** Bills passed by the Assembly by making "an order prohibiting the Clerk from submitting the Bill for Royal Assent".

This is not, however, a form of challenge on grounds of lack of competence, which would be made by the Attorney General under s.112.

Instead, there are the following specific grounds on which this form of control can be exercised: that the Bill—

- would have an adverse effect on any matter which is not listed under any of the headings in Pt 1 of Sch.7 (or falls within any of the exceptions specified in that Part of that Schedule);

- might have a serious adverse impact on water resources in England, water supply in England or the quality of water in England;

- would have an adverse effect on the operation of the law as it applies in England; or

- would be incompatible with any international obligation or the interests of defence or national security.

The first ground is of course close to an assertion of lack of competence, but there is a subtle distinction: the ground is not that there was no competence, but that the Bill would have an adverse affect on a matter with which it does not deal directly but which is outside legislative competence.

4.4.14 The potential importance of this provision is open to discussion. Some commentators in Wales have argued that it should not be under-estimated; others believe that in practice the power is unlikely to be exercised. Referring an Assembly Bill to the Supreme Court under s.112 is of course a politically aggressive action, but one can see that it has its place in the scheme of things. In essence, it recognises the distinction between legal effect and potential impact: a Bill might have no formal connection with an area of law that is outside legislative competence, but still have an unavoidable impact on that area. Section 114 is designed to allow impacts on matters outside competence to be prevented.

Since this process is not about competence and does not engage the fundamental proposition of s.108(2) that an Act of the Assembly is not law if it is outside competence, the process is available only in accordance with the statutory conditions which include, in particular, a 4 week deadline from passing of the Bill (or from reconsideration or from the decision of the Supreme Court on a challenge): s.114(4).

Section 114(5) provides that:

> "The Secretary of State must not make an order in relation to a Bill if the Secretary of State has notified the Clerk that no order is to be made in relation to the Bill."

An order under s.114 is made by statutory instrument and subject to negative resolution in Parliament—so it could be forced through against a majority of the Welsh Assembly, but not against a majority in Parliament.

The power under s.114 has not yet been exercised.

Section 154—Presumption of competence

There is a statutory presumption of competence, in effect, for any provision of an **4.4.15**
Act or Bill "which could be read in such a way as to be outside the Assembly's
legislative competence".

Section 154(2) requires that "the provision is to be read as narrowly as is
required for it to be within competence . . . , if such a reading is possible, and is
to have effect accordingly."

Perpetual challenge to legislative competence

Because of the strength of the proposition in s.108(2) of the 2006 Act, any **4.4.16**
provision of an Act of the Assembly that was outside the Assembly's legislative
competence when enacted is simply not law.

It follows, therefore, that even when all the procedures described above have
been exhausted and the Royal Assent has been given to an Act, it will fall away
if it can be demonstrated that it was not within legislative competence.

The most promising line for a person affected by an Act of the Assembly who
wishes to challenge it on the grounds that it was never within competence will
often be s.108(6) of the 2006 Act which provides that a provision is outside
legislative competence if "it is incompatible with the Convention rights or with
EU law."

But it will also be possible to argue that the subject fell outside the sphere of
devolved competence, which will be a particularly fruitful line to pursue when,
as so often happens, a provision can be seen as dealing with two subjects, one
within competence and one without, and it is necessary to decide whether the
former is necessarily incidental to the latter.

Remedial Orders

Section 151 of the 2006 Act allows the UK Government to make provision in **4.4.17**
consequence of a provision passed by the National Assembly being found to be
outside legislative competence.

Section 151 says as follows:

"(1) Her Majesty may by Order in Council make such provision as Her
Majesty considers appropriate in consequence of—

(a) an Assembly Measure or Act of the Assembly, or any provision of an
Assembly Measure or Act of the Assembly, which is not, or may not
be, within the Assembly's legislative competence, or

(b) any purported exercise by any person of a function conferred or
imposed by or under an Assembly Measure or Act of the Assembly
which is not, or may not be, an exercise or proper exercise of that
function.

(2) An Order in Council under this section may make such modifications of—

(a) any enactment (including any enactment comprised in or made under this Act) or prerogative instrument, or

(b) any other instrument or document, as Her Majesty considers appropriate.

(3) An Order in Council under this section may make provision having retrospective effect."

Retrospective effect of lack of competence decisions

4.4.18 Where a court or tribunal decides that an Act of the Assembly, or any provision of an Act of the Assembly, is outside the Assembly's legislative competence, it may make an order under s.153(2) of the 206 Act—

(a) removing or limiting any retrospective effect of the decision, or

(b) suspending the effect of the decision for any period and on any conditions to allow the defect to be corrected.

The court or tribunal must consider the extent to which persons who are not parties to the proceedings would otherwise be adversely affected by the decision.[140]

Subordinate legislation

4.4.19 Subordinate legislation can be made by Welsh Ministers under powers delegated by an Act or Measure of the Assembly, or in some cases by an Act of Parliament that confers powers on the Welsh Ministers in respect of the application of the Act to Wales.

The Assembly procedures for subordinate legislation are set out in Standing Order 27. The most common procedure for the scrutiny of subordinate legislation is the negative resolution procedure under which the legislation is "subject to annulment" in accordance with the enabling provision. The draft affirmative procedure, requiring approval of the National Assembly before the legislation is made, is also used.

Some statutory instruments fall to be made jointly by Welsh Ministers and Ministers of the Crown; it is common for those instruments to require to be laid both before the National Assembly and before Parliament.

---

[140] Section 153(3).

The figures for Welsh statutory instruments made in each year since 1999 are as follows:

1999	30
2000	123
2001	244
2002	212
2003	217
2004	192
2005	192
2006	222
2007	215
2008	181
2009	191
2010	170
2011	325
2012	325
2013	321
2014	350

PRIMARY LEGISLATION

SECTION 1

PREPARATION

Responsibility for the drafting of Bills

[Add to note 6]   **5.1.2**

The single-option Bill on fox-hunting was reintroduced the following Session and received Royal Assent under the provisions of the Parliament Acts (see para.5.2 51).

[Add to note 7]

Standing Orders also allot specified numbers of days for the consideration of the Estimates and for business selected by the Backbench Business Committee.

[Add after first sub-paragraph (ending " . . . to secure the passage of the Bill.")]   **5.1.3**

A private Member's or private peer's Bill may be drafted by a pressure group anxious to secure the passage of the Bill, or by the Clerks in the Public Bill Office of the relevant House. The Clerks are not lawyers, and aim to produce a text which is an adequate vehicle for a second reading debate but may not be a workable piece of legislation. Pressure groups that are anxious for their Bill—or amendments to a Government Bill—to pass into law will be at pains to ensure that the drafting is technically competent so that the Government cannot dismiss it simply on grounds that it will not work in its form as presented to Parliament.[12a]

[12a] See, for example: "With the assistance of the British Lung Foundation, I took the precaution of asking Daniel Greenberg to draft this amendment with me. I did so not simply because he is the editor of *Craies on Legislation, Stroud's Judicial Dictionary, Jowitt's Dictionary of English Law*, Westlaw UK Annotated Statutes and editor-in-chief of the *Statute Law Review*, but perhaps most importantly because he was parliamentary counsel from 1991 to 2010. Clearly, he knows a thing or two about drafting legislation, and presumably the Government would not cast doubt on the viability of the reams of legislation that he drafted for them."—Lord Alton, Mesothelioma Bill HL Deb, July 17, 2013 c.771.

Many private Members present a Bill without expecting it to pass into law and with the idea simply of furthering a publicity campaign; although the Bill is formally ordered to be printed, in many cases of presentation Bills of this kind no text is subsequently published, and accordingly the Bill exists only in the form of its long and short titles.

The legislative programme

5.1.5   [*Replace third sub-paragraph beginning "The present terms of reference . . . "*]

The present terms of reference of the Parliamentary Business and Legislation Committee are: "To consider issues relating to the government's Parliamentary business and implementation of its legislative programme."

[*Replace note 22*]

Membership of the Parliamentary Business and Legislation Committee is as follows: Leader of the House of Commons and Lord Privy Seal (Chair); Deputy Leader of the House of Commons (Deputy Chair); Secretary of State for Northern Ireland; Secretary of State for Scotland; Secretary of State for Wales; Chief Secretary to the Treasury; Leader of the House of Lords and Chancellor of the Duchy of Lancaster; Minister of State, Cabinet Office and Minister for Government Policy; Minister of State, Department for Education/Cabinet Office; Minister without Portfolio (currently the Conservative Party Chairman); Parliamentary Secretary to the Treasury and Chief Whip; Attorney General; Minister of State, Department for Environment, Food and Rural Affairs; Captain of the Gentlemen-at-Arms and Chief Whip (House of Lords); Deputy Leader of the House of Lords and Minister of State, Ministry of Justice; Deputy Chief Whip (Comptroller of HM Household); Captain of the Queen's Bodyguard of the Yeomen of the Guard and Deputy Chief Whip (House of Lords); Advocate General for Scotland. The First Parliamentary Counsel and Parliamentary Private Secretaries to the Prime Minister and Deputy Prime Minister are invited to attend.

5.1.7   [*Insert at end of note 28*]

; note that it is technically possible in the House of Lords to expand the scope of a Bill in the limited sense of instructing the Committee which considers it that it may include matters which are cognate to the purposes of the Bill but not otherwise within its field of relevance—see, for example, Local Audit and Accountability Bill [Lords] (Instruction) *http://www.publications.parliament.uk/ pa/cm201314/cmhansrd/cm131028/debtext/131028-0003.htm#13102830000002*; the same process can be carried out in the House of Commons, again only in relation to cognate matters—see, for example, the Motion passed on November

25, 2014 in relation to the Control of Horses Bill (private Member's); Motions of this kind are very rare in either House (amendments to the Long Title are slightly more common, and do not affect scope or relevance).

SECTION 2

PASSAGE OF PUBLIC BILL THROUGH PARLIAMENT
NORMAL PROCEDURE

Introduction

[Add to note 40]   **5.2.1**

The current edition of Erskine May is the 24th edn, published in 2011.

Status of Bill

[New paragraph]   **5.2.2.1**

The lack of a formal status of a Bill as an embryonic law does not mean that the courts today will not in certain cases be prepared to rule on matters relating to Bills (something that would once have been thought to offend against the privilege of Parliament as encapsulated in art.9 of the Bill of Rights).[41a] In general terms, moreover, it may be said that the courts are more prepared than they once were to admit that a decision may affect, and by implication should have regard to the possibility of influencing, draft primary or secondary legislation.[41b]

Despite that, however, the fundamental proposition remains that the Government cannot change the law by merely announcing their intention to do so, and

---

[41a] See, for example: "11 The Channel Islands contend that the proposed clause would, if enacted, be unlawful under European Union law and invite me so to declare. If I do, it is unlikely that the draft clause will be included in the Finance Bill. If I do not, it will be; and if Parliament enacts the Bill containing the clause, it will become law with effect from 1 April 2012. This claim is striking in two respects. Not so long ago, the notion that a judge might interfere in the workings of Parliament in this manner would have been considered constitutionally improper; but in areas of law within the competence of the European Union in which the law of the European Union must ultimately prevail, all sides accept that I can and should determine the issue."—*R. (on the application of Minister for Economic Development of Jersey) v Revenue and Customs Commissioners*, QBD (Administrative Court), March 15, 2012.

[41b] See, for example: "[17] In this application the court can only be concerned with establishing the lawfulness of the current practices and policies of the PSNI and it is not the function of this court nor would it be appropriate for it to comment on draft legislation pending before the legislature. The determination of this court in relation of the present application may, however, have implications for those involved in considering the draft legislation. That would be the inevitable outcome flowing from a court decision establishing or declaring the current state of the law."—*Gaughran's Application for Judicial Review, Re* [2012] NIQB 88.

still less by merely announcing their intention to invite Parliament to do so (as to which they may or may not be successful).[41c]

Introduction

5.2.7 *[Amendment]*

The Order Paper is now called the Order of Business.

Committee Stage (Commons)

5.2.14 *[Replace first two sub-paragraphs]*

Almost all government Bills are subject to a programme motion (see para. 5.2.26), which makes provision for the committal of the Bill.

Special Standing Committees were abolished on the creation of Public Bill Committees, which have wider powers to call witnesses and receive written evidence; and the term "Standing Committee" is no longer used.

The Minister in charge of a government Bill is usually one of the witnesses giving evidence to the Public Bill Committee considering it. Evidence is not normally taken on the Finance Bill, Bills which are not programmed, Bills already passed by the House of Lords, or private Member's Bills.

5.2.15 *[Add to note 86]*

As a general rule, issues of scope and relevance are determined in practice by the Clerks rather than through a formal ruling of the Speaker of the House of Commons or from the Speaker or Leader of the House in the House of Lords; but for a rare occasion of the House of Lords disregarding their Clerks' advice that a specific amendment was not relevant to the subject matter of the Bill and should not be debated, see the Electoral Registration and Administration Act 2013 s.6: *Hansard*, HL Vol.742, col.491 (January 14, 2012): *http://www.publications .parliament.uk/pa/ld201213/ldhansrd/text/130114–0001.htm#1301145000426*.

[41c] See, for example, "5. Before dealing with the issues, one submission can be addressed immediately. Mr Andrew Sutcliffe Q.C., on behalf of the Serious Organised Crime Agency ('SOCA') made it clear that the Government intends to use the Crime and Courts Bill presently before Parliament retrospectively to reverse the decision in *Perry* (see *Hansard*, 14 January 2013, column 636) and that, on the basis that the Spanish court gave effect to the property freezing order ('PFO'), there is every prospect that SOCA will be able to recover the proceeds of the property subject to the civil recovery order. It is sufficient to note that legislative change has not, as yet, been effected; it is irrelevant to the issues of law that now fall to be determined: if authority is required for what seems to me to be a self evident proposition, it is to be found in *Willow Wren Canal Carrying Co Ltd v British Transport Commission* [1956] 1 All E.R. 567 per Upjohn J at 569E–G."—*Serious Organised Crime Agency v O'Docherty (aka Mark Eric Gibbons)* [2013] EWCA Civ 518.

[Add to note 88]

The system of programming is now set out in Standing Orders Nos 83A–83I.

[Add to note 92]   **5.2.17**

Another example is the Hunting Bill, HC Deb. September 15, 2004.

Report (Commons)

[Add to first sub-paragraph]   **5.2.18**

The "report" from the Committee on a Bill (either the Committee of the Whole House or the Public Bill Committee) is the text of the Bill incorporating any amendments made in the Committee; it is not a discussion of the merits or otherwise of the Bill.

Grouping and selection of amendments (Commons)

[Add to note 107]   **5.2.22**

Amendments tabled in Public Bill Committees remain starred for two days rather than one.

Queen's or Prince's Consent (Commons & Lords)

[Amendment to note 111]   **5.2.23**

Correction: The reference should be to W.A. 419, rather than 417.

[Add to note 113]

For another (particularly resonant) example of Second Reading Consent being required, see the Succession to the Crown Bill 2012–13.

[New paragraph]   **5.2.23.1**

The procedures associated with the signification of Queen's Consent were examined by the House of Commons' Political and Constitutional Reform Committee in its[114a] Eleventh Report of Session 2013–14. Nothing particularly startling was discovered or recommended; in essence, the existing system continues. The most significant change in procedural terms is probably the

---

[114a] *The impact of Queen's and Prince's Consent on the legislative process*—HC 784—March 26, 2014.

recommendation that all Consent should be signified at Third Reading, which will avoid the need to consider whether changes to the prerogative are sufficiently significant to require Second Reading Consent.

Programme motions (Commons)

5.2.27   [*Replace first sub-paragraph*]

Programming is now an established feature of Commons procedure, and is regulated by Standing Orders (Nos 83A–83I).

House of Lords procedure

5.2.45   [*Replace sub-heading*]

The House of Lords Select Committee on Delegated Powers and Regulatory Reform

Royal Assent

5.2.48   [*Add to note 181*]

The House of Lords now elects its own Speaker from among its members, but she still lacks the regulatory powers of the Commons Speaker.

Timing: general

5.2.52   [*Add to first sub-paragraph*]

Since 2010, Parliamentary Sessions have begun in May. Section 1(2) of the Fixed-Term Parliaments Act 2011 provides for the next general election to take place in May 2015.

[*Add to note 201*]

The Banking (Special Provisions) Bill of 2007–08 passed through all its stages in both Houses in three days (February 19–21, 2008).

Emergency Bills

5.2.52.1   [*New paragraph*]

For an example of an Emergency Bill taken through all its parliamentary stages in both Houses in two days, see the Mental Health (Approval Functions) Act 2012–13.[202a]

[202a] An irregularity was discovered in the way doctors were approved for the purpose of enabling them to make medical recommendations about admitting mentally disordered patients to hospital and detaining them for their own health or safety or for the protection of the public under the Mental Health Act 1983. Four health regions—North East, Yorkshire and Humber, West Midlands and East

Timing: carry-over of Bills

[Add to second sub-paragraph]   **5.2.53.1**

Carry-over is now an established procedure. Since Parliamentary Sessions now begin in May, the annual Finance Bill is regularly brought in towards the end of the Session and carried over to the new Session with a view to Royal Assent in July.

Private Members' and private peers' Bills

[Insert at end of note 222]   **5.2.55**

Despite this, there are recent examples of Bills passing significant stages on the nod: see, for example, the Mutuals' Deferred Shares Bill [Lords] being read a second time and committed to Public Bill Committee on January 9, 2015 (c.571), and the Specialist Printing Equipment and Materials (Offences) Bill read a second time and committed to a Public Bill Committee on October 17, 2014 (c.649).

[New paragraph to be inserted before 5.2.57.1]   **5.2.57.A1**

On September 2, 2013 the House of Commons Procedure Committee published its report into Private Members' Bills.[227a] The Committee considered a number of aspects of the procedures surrounding private Members' Bills. In particular, it deprecated the practice of the Government giving "handout" Bills to Members successful in the private Member's Bills to take through under the guise of private Members' Bills, on the grounds that this subverts the intention of the Ballot to preserve time for non-Government initiatives.[227b]

Midlands—were affected by the irregularity. The Act gave retrospective validation to approvals under the Mental Health Act 1983 so as to provide that detentions were retrospectively made lawful. One might think this was precisely the kind of legislation where thorough parliamentary scrutiny was of particular importance.

[227a] 2nd Report of 2013–14; HC 188.

[227b] "Yet over a period of many years the House and its members have allowed this aspect of its procedures—which is important in both practical and symbolic terms—to be devalued and degraded to the point at which it can now barely be said that it functions independently of the Executive. In the 2012–13 Session of Parliament, ten supposedly 'private Members' bills reached the statute book. No fewer than nine of those were Government hand-out bills—that is, pieces of legislation prepared by Government which it had not been able to find time for in its own legislative programme, so instead persuaded backbenchers to take through in time which the Standing Orders provide is for non-Government business. Meanwhile other, genuinely backbench, bills were 'talked out' by Government ministers, or backbenchers who may have been acting at the Government's behest, and the House denied the opportunity even to come to a decision on them."

Introduction

5.3.1   *[Add to note 232]*

A "back of the Chair" Bill is so called because the Member introducing the Bill waits at the back of the Speaker's Chair until called and then steps forward to present the Bill formally by handing it to the Clerk at the Table.

5.3.2   *[Add to third sub-paragraph]*

The Joint Committee on Consolidation Bills has a peer who has held a judicial appointment as its Chairman.

5.3.3   *[Replace first sentence]*

It is usual for a Consolidation Bill to be introduced in the House of Lords by a Minister in the Ministry of Justice on behalf of the Lord Chancellor and the Secretary of State for Justice.

Introduction of private Bill

5.4.3   *[Add to third sub-paragraph]*

Private Bills proceed according to an annual cycle. Petitions are deposited in the House of Commons on or before November 27 in each year, unless the Chairman of Ways and Means grants permission for the deposit of a late petition. There are fixed dates by which notices must be publishes and other documents deposited. The Bills themselves—if the parliamentary requirements have been satisfied —are presented at the end of January.

Passage of private Bill

5.4.11   *[Add to second sub-paragraph]*

An opposed Bill committee is composed of four members including the chairman.

PART (3)

HYBRID BILLS

[New paragraph] **5.4.16.1**

An extensive discussion of the history and process of hybrid Bills was included in the judgments of the Supreme Court in an early challenge to the Bill for the HS2 development on European Union legislative compliance grounds.[287a] An extract from the judgment is given in Extract 12A in the Appendix.

Introduction

[Add to note 290] **5.4.19**

The Oversea Superannuation Bill 1990–91 was also introduced as a hybrid Bill.

[287a] *R. (on the application of HS2 Action Alliance Ltd) v Secretary of State for Transport* [2014] UKSC 3.

CHAPTER 6

SUBORDINATE LEGISLATION

SECTION 1

PREPARATION OF SUBORDINATE LEGISLATION

Consultation

[New paragraph]   **6.1.3.2**

Since January 2013, the policy has been "one-in two-out". The Regulatory Policy Committee issues a periodic report on the operation of the policy and on other aspects of its work (including guarding against "gold-plating" when transposing European Union obligations).[14a]

Notification to European Commission

[Add to note 37]   **6.1.11**

See, for example: "This Order was notified in draft to the European Commission in accordance with Directive 98/34/EC of the Parliament and of the Council of 22 June 1998 laying down a procedure for the provision of information in the field of technical standards and regulations (OJ No L204, 21.7.98, p 37) as amended by Directive 98/48/EC (OJ No L217, 5.8.98, p 18)"—Hallmarking Act 1973 (Application to Palladium) Order 2009 (SI 2009/2040) Explanatory Note.

[14a] For the Report on progress during the 2010–2015 Parliament see: *https://www.gov.uk/ government/uploads/system/uploads/attachment_data/file/415102/2015_03_03_RPC_Annual_ Report_2014_website_copy_revised_2015_03_19.pdf.*

SECTION 2

PARLIAMENTARY SCRUTINY

Affirmative resolution

6.2.2.1 *[New paragraph]*

There is a temptation for the courts and other readers to attach either too much or too little significance to the process of draft affirmative resolution. It is true that affirmative resolution means that the legislature has turned its figurative mind to the proposed exercise of the enabling power and approved it by distinct legislative action: and to that extent it could be said that an instrument that has been approved by Parliament in draft deserves at least similar degree of deference and presumption of lawfulness, as do Acts of Parliament themselves. Against that, it should be remembered that in practice the scrutiny of affirmative resolution instruments is generally perfunctory in the extreme, rarely descends to detail, is normally taken partly or wholly off the floor of each Chamber and is therefore without participation of the Houses as a whole and without any opportunity for line-by-line scrutiny and the making of amendments. Although, of course, the same could be said for much of the scrutiny of Acts of Parliament themselves. (In both instances, part of the problem is that judges are generally insufficiently knowledgeable about the realities of parliamentary procedure. Therefore, they find it difficult to know how to appraise the legal consequences of political and procedural acts.[42a])

The result is that there is an element of tergiversation or equivocation in the judicial attitude towards affirmative instruments. Perhaps the best summary offered by the judges themselves is that the courts will and should apply an element of caution in approaching a challenge to an affirmative instrument that is sufficient to outweigh or at least significantly qualify the presumption against

---

[42a] For a particularly striking example of judicial ignorance of parliamentary practicalities see: "36. On 2 July 2013 the Secretary of State decided 'in principle' to certify the appellant's judicial review proceedings pursuant to s.2C(1)(a) of the Special Immigration Appeals Commission Act 1997 (inserted by s.15 of the Justice and Security Act 2013, which came into force on 25 June 2013). The effective consequence will be that the judicial review will be transferred to SIAC which will be able to receive both open and closed evidence. The transfer has not yet taken place, because the 2003 Procedure Rules need to be amended to accommodate this new procedure, and that requires approval by the Joint Committee on Statutory Instruments and the affirmative resolution procedure in Parliament. We expressed the hope at the hearing on 16 July 2013 that counsel would agree any appropriate directions relating to the future conduct of the judicial review and the appeal against the deprivation decision. We anticipate that they will be heard by SIAC in tandem. The matter should be mentioned when our judgments in this appeal are handed down."—*L1 v Secretary of State for the Home Department* [2013] EWCA Civ 906.

delegation that will characterise their approach to other kinds of subordinate instrument.[42b]

[New paragraph] **6.2.3.1**

In Parliamentary terms one of the most significant reasons for requiring affirmative resolution for the exercise of a particular power is simply to make sure that it cannot pass "under the radar" of political notice. There are so many hundred negative resolution instruments made each year that it is easy to slip highly significant changes of the law into the pile without anyone noticing; the rigours of an affirmative resolution debate at least ensure that politicians focus on its substance, even if little or nothing in the way of substantive debate ensues.[46a]

[Insert new note 71a at end of paragraph] **6.2.11**

[71a] But for a rare example of a commencement order subject to affirmative resolution see the Defence Reform Act 2014 s.50, introduced by the following Ministerial statement—"On government

---

[42b] See, for example: "38. The Regulations were approved by Parliament by affirmative resolution in each House. Whilst it is common ground that this is of itself no bar to judicial review, it is an important feature of the case which we must bear firmly in mind. In *Bank Mellat v HM Treasury* [2013] 3 W.L.R. 179 at 239 Lord Sumption JSC said this: 'when a statutory instrument has been reviewed by Parliament, respect for Parliament's constitutional function calls for considerable caution before the courts will hold it to be unlawful on some ground (such as irrationality) which is within the ambit of Parliament's review. This applies with special force to legislative instruments founded on considerations of general policy'. 39. In *Preddy v Bull* [2012] 1 W.L.R. 2514 and *Black v Wilkinson* [2013] 1 W.L.R. 2489, both cases concerned with the Equality Act (Sexual Orientation) Regulations 2007, the Court of Appeal made similar observations, emphasising that the courts should respect the recent and closely considered judgment of a democratic assembly. 40. .Mr Wise pointed out that the 2012 Regulations had not been debated on the floor of the House of Commons (being approved on a division without debate); and that, as with all statutory instruments, the House could only accept or reject the regulations, with no opportunity for amendment. Indeed the Joint Committee on Human Rights observed that the affirmative resolution procedure presented only a limited opportunity for Parliamentary scrutiny. But that does not undermine the force of Lord Sumption's observation; and in the present case this point is in any event rather formalistic. The Welfare Reform Bill itself had been debated at length in both Houses. When the Public Bill Committee in the House of Commons considered clause 93 (which became section 96 of the Act) the very issues which have been raised before us were explored—for example whether child benefit or housing benefit should be excluded from the cap so as to mitigate the effect on large families. Whilst this parliamentary history is not a conclusive answer to the claimants' arguments—and Mr Eadie did not submit that it is—it is an important consideration. As Lord Bingham of Cornhill observed in *R (Countryside Alliance) v A-G* [2008] A.C. 719 at [45] 'the democratic process is liable to be subverted if, on a question of moral and political judgment, opponents of the Act achieve through the courts what they could not achieve in Parliament'. The same applies to questions of economic and political judgment."—*R (on the application of JS) v Secretary of State for Work and Pensions* [2013] EWHC 3350 (QB).

[46a] "Mr Hanson: I have been a Minister and the hon. Gentleman has been in opposition. He will know that part of the process of government and opposition is to ensure that there is scrutiny. Part of the problem of opposition is knowing when these matters have been laid and keeping on top of that information. First and foremost, we have to determine that an order has been laid and that it is something we need to consider and pray against. That is something that Oppositions can miss. This has been done in the past on his side and on our side. A substantive, affirmative resolution on such important issues as who is being removed from this country as a family member and other matters, could potentially be subject to affirmative resolution, which would ensure that they were considered formally, without the need to pray against them."—Immigration Bill 2013–14 PBC c.138.

Amendment 24, which I have already described, it is appropriate that Parliament has an opportunity further to debate the provisions in Part 1 at a point before they are commenced. I have tabled the amendment to allow this. It requires that both Houses approve by affirmative resolution a statutory instrument to commence the provisions in Part 1."—*http://www.publications.parliament.uk/ pa/ld201314/ldhansrd/text/140203-gc0001.htm#14020310000089.*

Hybrid instruments

6.2.23   [*Insert at end of note 134*]

; see also—"In earlier discussions, the hon. Gentleman noted that the Delegated Powers and Regulatory Reform Committee commented specifically on the provision. To clarify, the Committee did not raise concerns about its inclusion in the Bill, but noted that such a provision is usually accompanied by a commitment to consult affected parties, in place of the usual protections afforded by the hybrid procedure. Baroness Hanham, in the other place, made such a commitment in the Government's response to the Committee report and I committed to doing so when we debated amendment 76 last week. I am happy to repeat that commitment today: I confirm that we fully intend to consult all affected parties should such an order become necessary. As the hon. Gentleman outlined, such provisions are common practice, and as Baroness Hanham said in the other place, we expect the need to bring forward regulations that would affect bodies with both public and private functions to be rare. As with other legislation, it is sensible to include appropriate protection to ensure that if such regulations are needed in future, they are dealt with proportionately." See *http://www. publications.parliament.uk/pa/cm201314/cmpublic/localaudit/131121/am/ 131121s01.htm.*

6.2.23A   [*New paragraph*]

Although disapplication of the hybrid procedure is coming to be treated by the legislature as a matter of course, that does not mean that it will always be treated by the courts as being a matter for the legislature alone. There is evidence that the courts will consider the effect of de-hybridising provisions, or procedures having similarly limited effects, in contexts where the ability to challenge and influence legislation may be relevant to its efficacy or even validity.[134a]

[134a] See, for example: "143. Under the hybrid instrument procedure the instrument is subject to a procedure which enables those who are affected by the instrument to present arguments against it to a select committee which reports on its merits and recommends whether or not it should be approved: *Erskine May*, p 684. The disapplication of this procedure by an express provision of this kind is said to be relatively common in recent times: *Craies on Legislation* (10th ed, 2012), para 6.2.23. Nevertheless it is feature of the procedure under Part 4 of the Schedule that it has expressly excluded the possibility of consultation before the order is made. It excludes the possibility of presenting arguments against the order prior to its receiving approval in either House."—*Bank Mellat v Her Majesty's Treasury (No.2)* [2013] UKSC 39.

DEVOLVED LEGISLATION

SECTION 3

THE NATIONAL ASSEMBLY FOR WALES

[Replaces the existing text in Section 3]   **7.3.1**

Introduction

Section 111 of the Government of Wales Act 2006 sets the basic required stages for the consideration of Bills in the National Assembly:

"(1) The standing orders must include provision—

(a) for general debate on a Bill with an opportunity for Assembly members to vote on its general principles,

(b) for the consideration of, and an opportunity for Assembly members to vote on, the details of a Bill, and

(c) for a final stage at which a Bill can be passed or rejected.

(2) Subsection (1) does not prevent the standing orders making provision to enable the Assembly to expedite proceedings in relation to a particular Bill.

(3) The standing orders may make provision different from that required by subsection (1) for the procedure applicable to Bills of any of the following kinds—

(a) Bills which restate the law,

(b) Bills which repeal or revoke spent enactments, and

(c) private Bills.

(4) The standing orders must include provision for securing that the Assembly may only pass a Bill containing provisions which would, if contained in a Bill for an Act of Parliament, require the consent of Her Majesty or the Duke of Cornwall if such consent has been signified in accordance with the standing orders.

(5) The standing orders must include provision for securing that the Assembly may only pass a Bill if the text of the Bill is in both English and Welsh, unless the circumstances are such as are specified by the standing orders as any in which the text need not be in both languages.

(6) The standing orders must provide for an opportunity for the reconsideration of a Bill after its passing if (and only if)—

(a) the Supreme Court decides on a reference made in relation to the Bill under section 112 that the Bill or any provision of it would not be within the Assembly's legislative competence,

(b) a reference made in relation to the Bill under section 112 is withdrawn following a request for withdrawal of the reference under section 113(2)(b), or

(c) an order is made in relation to the Bill under section 114.

(7) The standing orders must, in particular, ensure that any Bill amended on reconsideration is subject to a final stage at which it can be approved or rejected.

(8) References in subsections (4), (5) and (6) of this section and sections 107(2), 109(5) and 116(3) to the passing of a Bill are, in the case of a Bill which has been amended on reconsideration, to be read as references to its approval."

Standing Orders—the four stages

7.3.2   The National Assembly has passed Standing Orders setting out the procedures for the passage of Public Bills.[56] The essence is a four-stage process that generally includes the following.

Stage 1—Consideration of General Principles

Stage 1 consists of consideration of the general principles of the Bill by a subject-based committee; the committee focuses on the main purpose of the Bill, leaving the detail to later stages. Committees can invite representations from interested parties, and may take written and oral evidence. Following the Committee's report, the Assembly considers and approves the general principles of the Bill.

Stage 2—Detailed Consideration by Committee

Stage 2 is the detailed consideration of a Bill, also generally in a subject-based committee. The committee considers any amendments proposed by Assembly Members.

---

[56] See Standing Order 26.

Stage 3—Detailed Consideration by the Assembly

Stage 3 is another detailed consideration stage, this time in plenary session of the National Assembly. Again, amendments are considered (subject to the Presiding Officer's power of selection).

Stage 4—Final Stage

Stage 4 is another stage taken in plenary session of the Assembly, and involves consideration of the Bill overall, as amended during its passage where relevant.

There is also provision under Standing Orders for a Report Stage between Stages 3 and 4[57]; this could be used to make adjustments to reflect competence concerns, for example—but to date it has not been invoked.

There is also provision under Standing Orders for a Reconsideration stage of a Bill that has been passed by the National Assembly but that has been referred to the Supreme Court on competence grounds.[58]

Introduction of Bills

The majority of Bills are introduced into the National Assembly by Welsh Government Ministers. **7.3.3**

Bills may also be introduced by Assembly committees, by the Assembly Commission, or by a backbench Assembly Member who has been successful in the ballot for the right to introduce a Bill.

On introduction the text of a Bill must be available in English and Welsh. The text must be accompanied by an Explanatory Memorandum setting out its policy objectives, details of any consultation undertaken on the Bill, estimates of the costs of implementing the Bill and other relevant information.

The Presiding Officer must publish a statement on introduction that the Assembly has legislative competence in relation to the subject-matter of the Bill.

Royal Assent

Once a Bill has been approved at stage 4 by the National Assembly, it must be presented to the Sovereign for Royal Assent.[59] **7.3.4**

The Clerk of the Assembly is responsible for submission of Bills for Royal Assent.

---

[57] Standing Order 26.45.
[58] Standing Order 26.52.
[59] Section 115.

There is an interval between stage 4 approval and Royal Assent, generally of at least four weeks, designed to leave time for any challenges by the Attorney General or Counsel General on competence grounds.

Private Acts

7.3.5 The National Assembly has the power to consider private Bills, within the Assembly's area of legislative competence, which are promoted by private individuals or organisations in order to obtain powers in excess of, or in conflict with, the general law. This is broadly the same jurisdiction as the Westminster Parliament has in relation to private Bills for Acts of Parliament brought by local authorities or other private organisations.

The procedure is set out in Standing Orders made by the National Assembly.[60]

As for private Bills in Westminster, the emphasis on private Bills in the Assembly is for the promoter to prove its case, in the sense of demonstrating that legislation is both necessary in order to achieve the stated policy and appropriate in all the circumstances (including other people's interests).

Also as in Westminster, the private Bill process allows objectors to show why the Bill should not be passed, and to that extent the proceedings on a private Bill can have an adversarial character. The focus of these proceedings is on the scrutiny committee procedure.

---

[60] See Standing Order 26A.

CHAPTER 8

DRAFTING LEGISLATION

SECTION 1

GENERAL PRINCIPLES

Plain English

[New paragraph]   **8.1.5.1**

It is important to note in the context of any discussion of the plain language movement in legislative drafting, that like all other deliberate changes of practice it may have unintended consequences in terms of judicial and other reactions. We can control how we draft, although we have limited control over how people perceive the results and give effect to them. Particularly obvious attempts at modernity in language are likely to be noticed by the judges, but they may attribute intentions to them that were not precisely the intent of the drafter.[25a]

It is also a sobering thought that what we see as praiseworthy simplicity in drafting can create or contribute to difficulties of interpretation. It is decades since Lord Renton warned in his eponymous report that citizens might be forced to litigation for the want of a few additional words; and the lesson does not appear to have been uniformly learned.[25b]

[25a] See, for example: "Parliament's use in section 20(3) of the Equality Act 2010 (set out in paragraph 25 above) of the plain English word 'puts', rather than the legal terms 'causes', is a signal that the court should adopt a practical and purposive approach to this provision. So the court should interpret and apply section 20(3) in such a way that the court's review of the defendant's compliance with the duty to make reasonable adjustments is a real and effective one. The interpretation preferred by Lewison LJ prevents that review taking place and so does not achieve that result."—*Firstgroup Plc v Paulley* [2014] EWCA Civ 1573.

[25b] See, for example: "S17 CA 1989's somewhat spurious clarity has already necessitated the assistance of both the Court of Appeal and the House of Lords in interpreting its proper construction. In my judgment the judge found himself in similar difficulty in relation to this issue; the wording is equivocal and does not, on its own, provide an answer to the question of whether a local authority has the power to provide services outside its area where a child in need has left the area voluntarily. . . . In all the circumstances therefore I endorse the judge's finding that the power under section 17(1) is, as the claimant claims, 'capable of being exercised outside the area of the local authority and at a time when the child himself is outside their area'."—*R. (on the application of J) v Worcestershire CC* [2014] EWCA Civ 1518.

Inclusion of inert material

8.1.13A   *[New paragraph]*

An increasing trend in statutory drafting involves the inclusion of material which is not merely declaratory or which may have clarificatory rather than substantive effect, but which is intended to have no effect at all other than to aid navigation.

Overview clauses, discussed below,[57a] are a specific example, but one that is relatively contained and understood. Much more troubling is the outbreak of italicised notes in the middle of operative provisions of statutory instruments.[57b] These are used increasingly to contain explanatory material of a kind that would be helpful in Explanatory Notes and is enormously dangerous scattered throughout the instrument itself. There are two principal sources of danger in this respect: first, that the courts will not know to what extent they should give some kind of interpretative weight to these provisions[57c]; and, secondly, that the reader will inevitably feel able to rely on the explanations and will therefore come to be misled significantly by inadvertent omissions or insufficient descriptions.

The Joint Committee on Statutory Instruments explored the issue of inert material in its First Special Report of Session 2013–14[57d]:

"2. We are aware that there are examples of primary legislation containing inert content for the purposes of elucidation. Thus the whole of Part 1 of the Income Tax Act 2007 appears to be of this nature. Primary legislation is not our remit, even if it provides Departments with a starting point for drafting secondary legislation. However, during the 2010–12 session, we noted that this practice had spread somewhat randomly into secondary legislation in ways that indicated that insufficient thought might have been given to the extent to which, if at all, it might be appropriate for secondary legislation.

[57a] At para.8.1.21.3.

[57b] A prime example is the statutory instruments containing Criminal Procedure Rules—see, for example, the Criminal Procedure Rules 2013 (SI 2013/1554 (L.16)). Rule 2.4 (representatives) is followed by an italicised note in square brackets in the following terms: "[Note. See also section 122 of the Magistrates' Courts Act 1980(32). A party's legal representative must be entitled to act as such under section 13 of the Legal Services Act 2007(33). Section 33(6) of the Criminal Justice Act 1925(34), section 46 of the Magistrates' Courts Act 1980(35) and Schedule 3 to that Act(36) provide for the representation of a corporation. Sections 3 and 6 of the Prosecution of Offences Act 1985(37) make provision about the institution of prosecutions. Section 223 of the Local Government Act 1972(38) allows a member or officer of a local authority on that authority's behalf to prosecute or defend a case before a magistrates' court, and to appear in and to conduct any proceedings before a magistrates' court. Part 7 contains rules about starting a prosecution.]" It is most improbable that this contains all the possibly relevant material on the subject, but readers are likely to assume quite reasonably that it does.

[57c] As in the case of the Explanatory Notes to Acts, a mere assertion that they have no authority will rightly be regarded by the courts as pre-judging an issue that is for them to determine.

[57d] HL 6; HC 167; May 21, 2013.

We considered that it might also give rise to confusion on the part of readers.

3. For example, in our 17th Report of the 2012–13 session, in respect of the Draft Universal Credit Regulations 2013, we commented on a provision described by the Department responsible as having no direct legal effect, but acting as aid to navigating the instrument. We said:

> The Committee deprecates the use of legislative text of an instrument, which by its nature should have—and is expected by the reader to have—legal effect, for the purpose of accommodating material which is merely explanatory in character and which is acknowledged by the Department to have no legal effect".

. . .

The legislation that governs statutory instruments does not expressly specify what provisions in an instrument as published count as operative, and we therefore consider that clear presentational distinction between operative and inert material is essential.

In the Annex to this Report we give a number of examples of our dialogue with Government Departments in respect of statutory instruments since 2010, either where material included in text that appears operative has no legal effect, or where essential elements that should be found in text that appears operative are found instead elsewhere. We remain firmly of the opinion that Departments should remain constant in distinguishing provisions that need to be included in legislation from those that do not properly belong there. We have three main reasons:

> the justification for items to be included in provisions generally presented as operative (in other words, regulations, articles, rules and Schedules) in secondary legislation is that they should have a legal effect: it is the only thing that operative provisions alone can do;

> once non-essential items are entered into such provisions there could well be the unintended consequence that courts will treat them as operative; and

> it also becomes impossible to draw a consistent line between what is right and wrong to include, in particular to draw a line between information and advertisement.

8. We discount the explanation on the part of the Departments that they wish to make explanations readily accessible to the non-expert reader, commendable though that aim is. There are various ways of achieving that in secondary legislation, for example via:

> the Explanatory Memorandum printed with every SI subject to parliamentary procedure;

parts of the instrument generally recognised as inoperative provisions, such as footnotes, headings, Explanatory Notes and suitably presented brackets; and explanatory literature wholly separate from the SI.

These methods reduce confusion to other readers and the courts, and in the case of the final option, are likely to be more accessible to lay readers of secondary legislation than the instrument itself.

. . .

We take this opportunity to stress that we will continue to draw the special attention of Parliament to instances where we consider there has been blurring of material that should be included in operative provisions of legislation with those that should not. In particular, we consider that inert material, if included at all, should not be presented as if it were part of the operative text. Explanations should be provided in non-operative parts of the instrument or other documents, and drafting should be as precise as possible to minimise the need for amplification and the potential for confusion.

13. We also reiterate our view, subject to the qualification indicated in paragraph ten, that the auxiliary verb "will" should only be used in legislation if straight futurity calls for legal effect. It should not be otherwise used in provision presented as operative, as it creates uncertainty as to whether discretion or obligation is intended."

SECION 2

SPECIFIC ISSUES

Gender

8.2.8.3 *[New paragraph]*

The Government's reply to a Parliamentary debate on gender neutral drafting in the House of Lords in 2013 is set out in Extract 12B in the Appendix.

CHAPTER 9

ACCESS TO LEGISLATION

SECTION 1

IMPORTANCE OF ACCESS

Ignorance of the law is no excuse

[*New paragraph*]   **9.1.3**

Accessibility as a component of efficacy of legislation is of particular importance in areas where, because of human rights law or other issues, legislation has to be justified by reference to being itself "in accordance with the law".[11a]

SECTION 3

PUBLICATION OF SUBORDINATE LEGISLATION

Legislation of the Scottish Parliament and Administration

[*New paragraph*]   **9.3.5A**

Section 41 of the Interpretation and Legislative Reform (Scotland) Act 2010 imposes a duty on the Queen's Printer to publish instruments. The responsible

---

[11a] "For a measure to be 'in accordance with the law', the relevant law must be adequately accessible and foreseeable, i.e. formulated with sufficient precision to enable the individual, if need be with appropriate advice, to regulate his conduct; and to meet these requirements a law must indicate with sufficient clarity the scope of discretion conferred on the competent authorities and the manner of its exercise. In *S v United Kingdom*, having recited that test in somewhat fuller terms at para [95], the court went on to express doubts as to whether s.64 of PACE was sufficiently precise to meet the test, in providing that retained samples and fingerprints 'shall not be used . . . except for purposes related to the prevention or detection of crime, the investigation of an offence or the conduct of a prosecution'. But it noted that the issue was closely related in that case to the broader issue of whether the interference was necessary in a democratic society, and in view of its analysis of that broader issue it did not find it necessary to decide whether the 'in accordance with the law' test was met."—*R. (on the application of C) v Commissioner of Police of the Metropolis* [2012] EWHC 1681 (Admin).

authority is required to ensure that the Queen's Printer receives a certified copy of each Scottish statutory instrument as soon as practicable after the instrument is made. In the same way as for UK general statutory instruments, s.41 provides that "In proceedings against a person for an offence consisting of a contravention of a Scottish statutory instrument, it is a defence to prove that, at the date of the alleged contravention, the instrument had not been published by the Queen's Printer."[74a]

SECTION 4

EXPLANATORY NOTES: BILLS AND ACTS

Review of the notes

9.4.10   [*New paragraph*]

On October 22, 2014 the Leader of the House of Commons issued a Written Ministerial Statement announcing a review of the form of Explanatory Notes for Bills and Acts, in the nature of a Pilot Scheme connected with the Armed Forces (Service Complaints and Financial Assistance) Bill [Lords].

> "The accompanying explanatory notes to this Bill pilot a new format which is easier to navigate and works better with online content. The notes now include:
>
> — A table of contents
> — A grid showing the application of each part of the Bill to each part of the United Kingdom
> — A shoulder note to the explanation of each clause and Schedule showing the application of the provision to each part of the United Kingdom
> — An explanation of both the policy and legal backgrounds, along with a summary of the existing law
> — An explanation of the financial implications of the Bill and of the need for a money resolution
> — Links to relevant policy documents
> — An explanation of how the measures in the Bill will be commenced
>
> The new format follows on from a review of explanatory notes which was conducted by the Cabinet Office and the Office of the Parliamentary Counsel as part of the Good Law project. In support of this work officials met with a variety of stakeholders and conducted an online survey which obtained views from within and beyond Parliament."

[74a] subs.(3).

CHAPTER 10

TIMING

SECTION 1

COMMENCEMENT

Status of legislation pending commencement

[*Add new note 7a at end of second sub-paragraph beginning "The simple answer... "*]   **10.1.2**

"An Act which has been enacted by both Houses of Parliament and has received the Royal Assent is on the statute book. But it does not follow that a provision of the Act is necessarily part of the law of the United Kingdom. As Hobhouse L.J. stated in *R. v Secretary of State for the Home Department, Ex p Fire Brigades Union* [1995] 2 A.C. 513, 529: "whether or not a provision becomes part of the law of the United Kingdom depends upon whether and when it comes into force: that is what coming into force means. When a statutory provision becomes part of the law of the United Kingdom depends upon what commencement provision Parliament has enacted. The same is true, mutatis mutandis, of statutes passed by the Scottish Parliament and the other devolved legislatures. The Interpretation Act 1978 ('the 1978 Act') provides in Sch.1, to which effect is given by s.5, that 'commencement', in relation to an Act or enactment, means the time when it comes into force. That provision applies to statutes enacted by the United Kingdom Parliament. In relation to Acts of the Scottish Parliament, a similar definition is contained in Sch.2 to the 1999 Order, and in Schedule 1 to the Interpretation and Legislative Reform (Scotland) Act 2010 ('the 2010 Act'), which has now replaced the 1999 Order. . . . Although most modern statutes favour the expression 'come into force', the expression 'come into operation' has also been used in the same sense, and was in more common use in earlier times. These expressions, and others such as 'speaks from ' and 'comes into effect ', have been used interchangeably by the courts, and are also used interchangeably in textbooks on statutory interpretation, such as . . . *Craies on Legislation*, 10th ed (2012). The latter states at para 10.1.1

that 'the terms 'commencement', 'coming into force', 'taking effect', 'coming into effect' and 'coming into operation' are interchangeable and mean no more than the time when the legislation starts to have legal effect '. . . . It follows that the distinction which the Ministers have sought to draw between a provision being in force, in the sense that it has become law, on the one hand, and its being in effective operation, on the other hand, is in principle a valid distinction. In a commencement provision such as section 333(2) of the 2003 Act, in particular, the words 'in force' can only bear the former of those senses. That is because the effect of a provision which fixes a date when provisions 'shall come into force' is that those provisions will automatically come into force on the specified date. Nothing requires to be done in order for the provisions to come into force beyond passively awaiting the date fixed by the Act itself. If however the provisions being brought into force cannot be brought into effective operation without further action being taken—as is true, on any view of the matter, of the provisions to which section 333(2) applies—then the commencement provision must be referring only to the bringing of the provisions into force as law, and not to their being brought into effective operation. That conclusion does not however permit one to infer, from a commencement provision in the form of section 333(2), that Parliament did not intend that the provisions to which it applies should be brought into effective operation on the date when they come into force. On the contrary: the inference which one would naturally draw, unless the contrary intention appears, is that that was indeed the intention of Parliament."—*RM v The Scottish Ministers (Scotland)* [2012] UKSC 58.

Presumption of immediate commencement

10.1.4   [*Insert at end of note 20*]

(Note that the invariable rule of express commencement for statutory instruments holds good only for substantive instruments; commencement orders and similarly technical instruments will not necessarily include express provision for their own commencement.)

Section 2

Duration

Fixed term or "sunset" clause

10.2.4A   [*New paragraph*]

Sunset clauses attract a surprising degree of controversy. At first sight it might seem a trite proposition that if a particular provision is justified by reference to circumstances that are or may be temporary, it follows that the provisions should be subject to a sunset clause, with or without the power to continue them before expiry by reference to, and on satisfactory demonstration of, continued justification. Despite that, governments routinely oppose the insertion of sunset clauses, perhaps simply as a reflex administrative objection to the need to monitor the effect of legislation and to justify its continuation; although governments are generally happy to undertake to monitor progress in relation to an Act, they are generally reluctant to commit to procedures that would require them to submit the monitoring, its extent, efficacy and results, to outside scrutiny.[119a]

Section 3

Retrospectivity

Vested interests

[New paragraph]   **10.3.7.1**

The policy of the presumption against retrospection is sometimes said to be the protection of vested interests.

That may be part of the purpose of the presumption but it is not all. In particular, the presumption applies at its strongest force to situations like retrospective criminality where there is no issue of vested private interests.

Apart from being incomplete as a reason for the presumption, the protection of vested interests as a concept rarely take the argument forward:

> "19. Ms Stevens-Hoare also relies strongly on the presumption against retrospective legislation. The presumption is said to arise when legislation removes or impairs a vested right. As Lord Hoffmann and Lord Brown pointed out in *Odelola v Secretary of State for the Home Department* [2009] UKHL 25, [2009] 1 W.L.R. 1230 at [5] and [31] respectively arguments of this kind are often circular, because they simply transfer attention to the question whether a person has a vested right which legislation will remove or impair. . . . 23. In my judgment in so far as section 215 (1) (a) precludes the service of a section 21 notice it is prospective in operation rather than retrospective. It is only concerned with section 21 notices served after it came into force. Had it invalidated section 21 notices served before it came

---

[119a] See, for example: "I am not going to agree to a sunset clause. It is absolutely right to examine how we monitor and review progress. The effect of such a clause would be for schedule 16 to cease to have effect five years after coming into force. That would be rigid. The Government consider the amendment to be unnecessary because of the measures that were outlined in the other place. We gave an undertaking that we will review the operation of the scheme following its introduction. In any event, we are committed to reviewing all new primary legislation within five years of Royal Assent in line with the Government's policy on post-legislative scrutiny."—Crime and Courts Bill 2012–13: *http://www.publications.parliament.uk/pa/cm201213/cmpublic/crimeandcourts/130205/pm/130205 s01.htm.*

into force, it would have been retrospective in its operation. But it does not."[160a]

Special case (2): tax

10.3.11   *[Insert at end of note 177]*

; see also: "76. Parliament was entitled to decide that this was a case in which there was justification for making the legislation retrospective. This was an exceptional situation in which, for the reasons I have stated, the amount of tax to be saved was of little or no significance compared with the need to reinforce the strength of the deterrent message and to confine the operation of s.45 to transactions which would give effect to Parliament's original intention. There was already a history of warnings and of measures being taken to close down similar artificial and abusive schemes. In the six weeks remaining before the new transfer of rights rules came into effect, there was reason to fear that more people would jump on the bandwagon in order to avail themselves of the potential loophole before it closed down for good. It did not matter how many or few people would actually do so; the Government was seeking to change such behaviour and to promote fairness among taxpayers."—*R. (on the application of St Matthews (West) Ltd) v HM Treasury* [2014] EWHC 1848 (Admin).

Retrospective validation

10.3.16.1   *[New paragraph]*

Where a piece of legislation turns out to be invalid or likely to be open to challenge on grounds of validity, the government and the legislature are likely to conclude that it is necessary to validate the original legislation and very often to do so with retrospective effect.

Whether that is proper will depend on all the circumstances and factors already discussed in this chapter. At one extreme, where the invalidity arises from a technical or formal irregularity that might have been expected to pass unnoticed and about which nobody could reasonably care, retrospective validation is unlikely to be controversial. At the other extreme, where the invalidity goes to the substance of the original legislation, a proposal to validate retrospectively is likely to be significantly controversial.

[160a] *Charalambous v NG* [2014] EWCA Civ 1604.

The proposal to legislative to validate retrospectively may still leave live issues around effect and validity that the courts will feel able to consider.[195a]

[195a] "This court, like other courts, is normally concerned with stating the law as it is, not as it was. Further, it is rather unattractive for the executive to be taking up court time and public money to establish that a regulation is valid, when it has already taken up Parliamentary time to enact legislation which retrospectively validates the regulation. That very point was made on behalf of Miss Reilly and Mr Wilson in order to oppose the Secretary of State's application for permission to appeal to this court, and, at least viewed from our present perspective, we consider that there was considerable force in the point. 41. However, permission to appeal has been given to the Secretary of State, the issue concerned is not the only point at stake in the appeal, the issue may be of some significance to the drafting of regulations generally, and the retrospectively validating legislation is under attack. Bearing in mind those factors, we are of the view that issue (a) should be considered, although the precise formulation of any order that is made will have to be carefully considered, bearing in mind the effect of the 2013 Act."—*R. (on the application of Reilly) v Secretary of State for Work and Pensions* [2013] UKSC 68.

EXTENT AND APPLICATION

Section 1

Extent

Sark

[New paragraph]   **11.1.8.2A**

The constitutional relationship of Sark to the United Kingdom and to the Crown is discussed further in the following terms in *Barclay v Secretary of State for Justice*[38a]:

"i) Sark is an island of about 600 people. It includes the island of Brecqhou which the claimants purchased in 1993. It is part of the Crown Dependency of the Bailiwick of Guernsey. Her Majesty is sovereign of the Bailiwick of Guernsey and the Bailiwick of Jersey (which comprise the whole of the Channel Islands), her predecessors having succeeded to the sovereignty of the islands from the Dukes of Normandy.

ii) The two Bailiwicks have a unique constitutional position. Neither is part of the United Kingdom nor a colony nor an overseas territory nor a state. Nor are the inhabitants represented in the UK Parliament. They have a right by royal grant to autonomous government which is respected by the UK Parliament. Laws enacted by the UK Parliament do not extend to them automatically, though the UK Parliament's right to legislate is paramount. By convention the UK Parliament does not legislate in purely domestic matters or tax.

iii) The UK Government is responsible for their international relations and for their defence; they cannot enter into international treaties.

[38a] [2013] EWHC 1183 (Admin).

iv) The Crown has ultimate responsibility for the good governance of the island, with the Secretary of State carrying within the UK Government that Departmental responsibility.

v) The Seigneur of Sark is the hereditary Lord of Sark, holding the island as a royal fief in succession to the first Seigneur who received the island in 1565. His family acquired the fief in 1852. He acts in a number of capacities to which it will be necessary to refer. He is a member of the Chief Pleas.

vi) The Seneschal has for many centuries been the judge of the court in Sark. Additional judges are appointed as Deputy Seneschals. The jurisdiction of the court is determined by Order in Council. Its procedure is Norman Customary law. The civil jurisdiction is unlimited. The criminal jurisdiction is limited to one month's imprisonment and a fine not exceeding level 4. An appeal from the Court of the Seneschal lies to the Royal Court of Guernsey with an appeal ultimately to the Privy Council. The workload of the court was described by the former Seneschal, Lt. Col. Guille, as being quite light. All the cases are comparatively simple.

vii) The Chief Pleas is not only the legislature of Sark, but also exercises powers of the Executive through its committees. The legislature of Guernsey requires the consent of the Chief Pleas to legislate for Sark, save in criminal matters where it can legislate without that consent.

viii) The Chief Pleas can pass two types of legislative measure—an Ordinance and a Law. The legislative competence of the legislature of Guernsey to make Ordinances without reference to Her Majesty was considered in the judgment of Lord Mance in *Jersey Fishermen's Association v States of Guernsey* [2007] UKPC 30.

ix) A Law, however, requires the approval of Her Majesty in Council. After the Chief Pleas has passed a Law, that Law is sent as a projet de loi through the Lieutenant Governor of Guernsey to the Ministry of Justice. Petitions in support of or against the Law can be lodged.

x) The Justice Committee of the House of Commons reported in March 2010 that the Secretary of State, as a member of the Committee and the Departmental Minister in the United Kingdom Government responsible for the affairs of the Channel Islands, can legitimately recommend that Royal Assent of legislative measures from the legislative bodies of the Channel Islands be withheld, if the legislation would put the Island in breach of an obligation which applies to the Island and for which the UK is responsible. The legislation of the Islands had to comply with international human rights obligations.

xi) Prior to the Privy Council making a decision to approve a Law, the Committee, comprising the Secretary of State, a Minister of State in the Ministry of Justice and the Lord President of the Council makes a recommendation to the Privy Council. The Committee was constituted by an Order in Council dated 22 February 1952 to receive all Laws passed by the Channel Island and petitions in respect of them. Where appropriate that Committee is advised by the Secretary of State. If approval is given, that is given by Her Majesty in Council by Order in Council.

xii) The evidence in *Barclay No 1* and before us was that the Committee will in general respect the decision of Chief Pleas. If a Law would violate the Crown's international obligations or any fundamental constitutional principle or would clearly violate the public interest, then the Committee might recommend withholding approval.

xiii) The Privy Council acts on the recommendation of the Committee; there is no substantive debate."

SECTION 2

PERSONAL APPLICATION

Application to persons abroad and to actions performed abroad

[New paragraph]   **11.2.5.1**

As with other presumptions of construction, the presumption against extraterritoriality will apply more strongly to forms of legislation which are greater intrusions than others into personal liberty.[55a]

SECTION 3

HUMAN RIGHTS

Introduction

[New paragraph]   **11.3.2A**

In addition to individual presumptions and canons of construction, there is a general principle of legality that has an autonomous United Kingdom meaning

---

[55a] See, for example: "However, he submitted that the language used fell short of indicating a clear intention by Parliament to confer exterritorial jurisdiction. This being a penal statute, he submitted that there was an element of uncertainty and made a contrast with the drafting style of the Criminal Justice Act 1993 as amended, which he said deals with jurisdiction in a more explicit way. 49.We do not dissent from that last proposition, but have come to the conclusion that there was jurisdiction to try this appellant based on the provisions we have referred to, and in particular those at Section 340(11)(d). Whilst the monies obtained by the fraud in the UK became criminal property once they reached a bank account in the UK controlled by the conspirators, those proceeds did not cease to be criminal property when they arrived in the appellant's bank account in Spain. By permitting the use of that bank account for receipt and then withdrawal of those monies, the appellant was converting them. We reject the argument that once the victims had been defrauded of their money and it had gone into the conspirators' UK bank account, there were no further consequences for the affected consumers."—*R. v Rogers (Bradley David)* [2014] EWCA Crim 1680.

and effect, and that extends into a number of areas also addressed by the European Convention on Human Rights.[72a]

Introduction

11.3.2.1 *[New paragraph]*

Even in cases where Convention Rights are engaged, the courts will keep an eye on the underlying constitutional principles and aim to develop the application of the Convention rights in accordance with the United Kingdom's fundamental principles of the rule of law.[72b]

[72a] See, for example:

"54. Ms Kaufmann and Ms Williams rely on the principle of legality. There was no issue between the parties on this principle. But it requires explanation. There is in fact more than one principle of legality. There is one at common law and one under the HRA.

55. The common law principle of legality assumes that the common law recognises fundamental rights, and that it did so before, and independently of, the HRA. The common law principle is that, in the absence of express language or necessary implication to the contrary, the courts presume that even the most general words in a statute were intended by Parliament to be subject to the basic or fundamental rights of the individual.

56. The principle was re-affirmed in *R v Secretary of State for the Home Department, Ex Parte Simms* [1999] UKHL 33, [2000] 2 A.C. 115. That case was decided after the HRA had been enacted and before it had come into force. The issue was whether a restriction on a prisoner's right to communicate orally with a journalist was an unlawful interference with the fundamental right of freedom of speech which is recognised by the common law. In a much cited passage Lord Hoffmann said at p131:

'Parliamentary sovereignty means that Parliament can, if it chooses, legislate contrary to fundamental principles of human rights. The Human Rights Act 1998 will not detract from this power. The constraints upon its exercise by Parliament are ultimately political, not legal. But the principle of legality means that Parliament must squarely confront what it is doing and accept the political cost. Fundamental rights cannot be overridden by general or ambiguous words. This is because there is too great a risk that the full implications of their unqualified meaning may have passed unnoticed in the democratic process. In the absence of express language or necessary implication to the contrary, the courts therefore presume that even the most general words were intended to be subject to the basic rights of the individual. In this way the courts of the United Kingdom, though acknowledging the sovereignty of Parliament, apply principles of constitutionality little different from those which exist in countries where the power of the legislature is expressly limited by a constitutional document'.

57. The separate principle of legality (see Simms p132A) is in the HRA s.3. It relates to those rights enshrined in the ECHR. The two categories (fundamental rights recognised at common law and ECHR rights) overlap, but are not identical. HRA s.11 ("Safeguard for Existing Human Rights") specifically provided that the HRA should not restrict reliance upon any other right or freedom having effect under English law. The HRA principle of legality is: . . . "—*AKJ v Commissioner of Police for the Metropolis* [2013] EWHC 32 (QB).

[72b] See, for example:

"82. Although these principles emanate from decisions of the ECtHR, in my view they also accurately reflect fundamental principles of the UK's unwritten constitution. The constitutional principle of the rule of law was expressly recognised in section 1, Constitutional Reform Act 2005. It requires, inter alia, that Parliament and the Executive recognise and respect the separation of powers and abide by the principle of legality. Although the Crown in Parliament is the sovereign legislative power, the Courts have the constitutional role of determining and enforcing legality. Thus, Parliament's undoubted power to legislate to overrule the effect of court judgments generally ought not to take the form of retrospective legislation designed to

The entrenchment of fundamental rights into the law of the United Kingdom leads to the presumption against encroachment upon them sometimes expressed as the principle of legality.[72c]

Incompatibility: primary legislation

[New paragraph]   **11.3.6.2**

If a party to legal proceedings seeks a declaration of incompatibility, there is a procedural requirement to notify the Government so that it can make representations if it wants to; and this procedural requirement will not generally be waived.[91a]

SECTION 5

THE CROWN

Express Crown application

[New paragraph]   **11.5.12.1**

The more common it becomes for the legislature to disapply the presumption against Crown application expressly, the more reluctant the courts become to infer disapplication from implication.[176a]

---

favour the Executive in ongoing litigation in the courts brought against it by one of its citizens, unless there are compelling reasons to do so. Otherwise it is likely to offend a citizen's sense of fair play."—*R. (on the application of Reilly) v Secretary of State for Work and Pensions* [2014] EWHC 2182 (Admin).

[72c] See further Ch.20.

[91a] "In any event, rule 19.4A(1) of the Civil Procedure Rules prohibits the court from making a declaration of incompatibility unless notice has been given to the Crown, and that has not been done."—*R. (on the application of Boots Management Services Ltd) v Central Arbitration Committee* [2014] EWHC 65 (Admin).

[176a] See, for example: "As already explained, the requirement of 'necessary implication' is well settled and not to be whittled down. We acknowledge readily that the CJA 2009 does not contain any express provision binding the Crown—by contrast with statutes such as the Senior Courts Act 1981 (s.35(4)) and the Inquiries Act 2005 (s.50). There is considerable force in the argument that when Parliament intends to bind the Crown it knows how to do so. We have such considerations well in mind when considering the CJA 2009."—*R. (on the application of Revenue and Customs Commissioners) v HM Coroner for Liverpool* [2014] EWHC 1586 (Admin).

The Duke and Duchy of Cornwall

11.5.25A   [*New paragraph*]

Recent changes in relation to Crown succession have had implications for the Duchy.[207a]

[207a] "The Sovereign Grant Act 2010 makes a very important change that touches on the succession to the Crown as far as the Duchy of Cornwall is concerned. As the hon. Member for North East Somerset (Jacob Rees-Mogg) may know, the convention is that the male heir to the throne has the title of Duchy of Cornwall conferred on him, but a female heir to the throne does not. The Bill does not change that situation, but the provisions of the Sovereign Grant Act mean that the financial support provided via the Duchy of Cornwall can, in future, be provided to female heirs to the throne as well. To that extent, there is a link between this very tightly circumscribed Bill and the provisions of the Sovereign Grant Act."—Deputy Prime Minister, Crown Succession Bill 2012–13, HC Deb., January 22, 2013, c.211.

STATUTORY RIGHTS, POWERS AND DUTIES

SECTION 1

CREATION AND REMOVAL

Presumption against interference with rights

[*Insert at end of note 8*]   **12.1.3**

; see also—"If there were any ambiguity as to the proper construction of the relevant provisions it could be resolved by examining the legislative provisions which were in place before the 1986 Act, and by application of the canon of construction which presumes that legislation does not intend to remove an existing right unless it does so expressly or by clear implication (*Craies on Legislation* (9th ed.), p.501; *Re Cuno* [1889] 43 Ch D 12, per Bowen LJ at 17)."—*M, Re For Enforcement Of A Residence Order* [2013] CSOH 160; 2013 S.L.T. 1043.

SECTION 2

NATURE OF POWERS AND DUTIES

Limitations on discretionary statutory power

[*Insert at end of note 52*]   **12.2.7.2**

; see also—"34. The judge's answer to the argument that the maxim generalia specialibus non derogant applies to preserve s.27 as the applicable power of sale was that the 1908 Act, properly construed, impliedly repealed s.27 in favour of s.32. But both are simply different views about the construction of s.32 of the 1908 Act in the absence of any express repeal of s.27 and the inconsistency between the two provisions in terms of when a sale will be permitted. One can present the arguments in a number of different ways by asking why s.27 was continued in effect if it was only to have concurrent application with s.32 rather than an exclusive one; whether Parliament can really have intended to remove s.27 protection from s.6(4) allotments; and whether the existence of the wide s.32 power which, on the express language of s.33(4), does apply to s.6(4) allotments suggests (as the judge found) that s.27 was to cease to have any further application to such land."—*Snelling v Burstow Parish Council* [2013] EWCA Civ 1411.

12.2.7.3 *[New paragraph]*

The Padfield principle is of increasing importance as primary legislation confers broader and broader powers in the shape of skeleton Bills that leave everything to be settled by Ministers in secondary legislation. Its modern importance has been recognised in a number of recent judicial decisions. See, for example:

> "The importance of *Padfield* was its reassertion that, even where a statute confers a discretionary power, a failure to exercise the power will be unlawful if it is contrary to Parliament's intention. That intention may be to create legal rights which can only be made effective if the power is exercised, as in Singh v Secretary of State for the Home Department. It may however be to bring about some other result which is similarly dependent upon the exercise of the power. Authorities illustrating that principle in the context of a statutory power to make regulations, where such regulations were necessary for the proper functioning of a statutory scheme, include *Greater London Council v Secretary of State for the Environment* [1984] JPL 424 and *Sharma v Registrar to the Integrity Commission* [2007] 1 W.L.R. 2849, para 26, per Lord Hope of Craighead. In the present case, the exercise of the power to make regulations by 1 May 2006 was necessary in order to bring Chapter 3 of Part 17 of the 2003 Act into effective operation by that date, as the Scottish Parliament intended. The Ministers were therefore under an obligation to exercise the power by that date."[52a]

For a modern judicial discussion of the application of Padfield principle, see *Haworth, R. (on the application of) v Northumbria Police Authority.*[52b]

The fact that the Padfield principle will be used by the courts to limit the ambit of provisions cast in unrestricted terms does not mean that it becomes politically acceptable to confer unlimited powers. Parliament increasingly presses the view that it is not constitutionally proper to confer wide powers and leave it to the courts to impose limitations on them. Equally, the fact that the Government are able to assert that their intention is not to make the fullest possible use of the

---

[52a] *RM v The Scottish Ministers (Scotland)* [2012] UKSC 58.
[52b] [2012] EWHC 1225 (Admin).

literal power is a reason for *not* legislating in such wide terms, not an excuse for doing so.[52c]

Equally, the courts will resist attempts to put them in the position of mending the deficiencies of Parliament in the sense of implying into broad powers particular limitations on restrictions that are more a matter of providing satisfactory substantive safeguards than of deducing the legislative intent.[52d]

SECTION 3

EXERCISE OF POWERS AND DUTIES

Time limits

[New paragraph]   **12.3.7**

Special considerations apply to the application of time limits:

[52c] See, for example: "The Government have repeatedly stated their policy intention only to designate planning authorities in exceptional cases. The explanatory notes speak of 'the intention being to make such designations where an authority has a record of very poor performance', while the consultation paperenvisages the power being exercised 'very sparingly'. Likewise, the minister, Nick Boles MP, spoke in the Public Bill Committee in the House of Commons of 'a very small number' of planning authorities being designated: 'fewer than 20'. At second reading in the House of Lords, the minister, Baroness Hanham, stated that 'we would be delighted if it were not necessary for any local authority to be designated under this clause'. We have consistently expressed the view that executive assurances about howstatutory powers will be exercised are no firm basis on which to legislate. Constitutionally speaking, they are no proper substitute for clarity in the statutory provision. In our view, the Government's own policy intention of designation under clause 1 only in exceptional cases should be made clear on the face of the bill. The House may also wish to consider whether the criteria and procedures for making or revoking a designation should be set out in secondary legislation."—Select Committee on the Constitution, 10th Report of Session 2012–13, Growth and Infrastructure Bill Report, January 18, 2013.

[52d] See, for example: "Section 17 says nothing about the consideration paid by a local housing authority for the acquisition. The case for Cornwall is that the power conferred by section 17 has to be read as a power to acquire at a reasonable price and that that requires those acting on behalf of the local housing authority to act in compliance with the fiduciary duty to council taxpayers. This, in turn, required the councils to have regard to market rents before entering into any commitment. . . . When one compares this case with the leading authorities in which the breach of fiduciary duty approach was propounded and in which it succeeded, it seems to me that the present facts, taken at their highest, establish significantly less culpability. There is no evidence of 'eccentric principles' or of 'flagrant violation' of the kind found in *Roberts v Hapwood*, or of 'the making of a gift or present' to CTE, to use the language of Prescott, or doubling of the ratepayers' burden as had occurred in the *Bromley* case. Nor was there the self-evident element of ultra vires that underlay *Credit Suisse* (see below, paragraph 29). In the present case, the attempt to present it as one of 'pure' ultra vires depends upon reading the words 'at a reasonable price' into section 17(1)(b) of the Housing Act 1985. There are two reasons for rejecting that approach. The first is that, in the absence of expert evidence, there is no basis for concluding that the rents were not 'a reasonable price' The second reason is more fundamental. In my judgment, it will rarely be appropriate to read into a statutory power a limitation defined by something such as a "reasonable price". To do so would be to invite judicialisation of the limits of legal capacity in the sense that capacity might be ascertainable only upon a judicial determination of the reasonableness of a price. It is surprising to see a local authority contending for that. It is something that courts are alert to avoid."—*Charles Terence Estates Ltd v Cornwall Council* [2012] EWCA Civ 1439.

"These cases indicate that a flexible approach must normally be taken to public law time limits. On occasion, failure to adhere to a time limit may invalidate all further procedure. In most cases, however, there will be no automatic invalidity. The purpose of the time limit, the legal and factual context in which it arises, and the practical consequences of failure to adhere to the time limit will always be important in determining whether there is invalidity. Other relevant matters will include the length of any delay, the question of whether delay has caused actual prejudice, and the existence or otherwise of good faith. In every case the critical question is whether the intention underlying the legislation was that a failure to observe the time limit in the particular circumstances of the case should result in total invalidity. The application of these principles is illustrated by two further cases to which we were referred. In *R v Soneji* [2006] 1 AC 340, the defendants had pled guilty to money laundering offences. The prosecutor then served notice to make a confiscation order in respect of the proceeds of criminal conduct. The prosecutor's notice, however, had been served approximately one week late, and the judge had not exercised power to extend the time limit on account of exceptional circumstances. It was held that the failure to comply with the time-limit did not render the prosecutor's notice invalid. The confiscation order had been made within the general timeframe contemplated by Parliament; thus the prejudice to the accused was not significant, and was decisively outweighed by the countervailing interest in not allowing a convicted offender to escape confiscation for bona fide errors in the judicial process: Lord Steyn at paragraph 24; Lord Rodger at paragraph 41. Furthermore, the provisions in question created a duty on the court to consider the making of a confiscation order; that duty was not to be frustrated by the failure to observe a time limit that caused no material unfairness: Lord Cullen at paragraph 57. There had been substantial performance, as the departure from the prescribed time limit was minor and no prejudice was created or injustice done: Lord Carswell at paragraph 67–68. These are all factors that can be spelled out of the earlier decisions."[72a]

SECTION 4

MINISTERIAL POWERS AND DUTIES

Policy decisions and operational decisions distinguished

12.4.12   *[New paragraph]*

As challenges to the exercise by the Executive of statutory functions have become more numerous and wider ranging, the courts have had to develop

---

[72a] *Shahid v The Scottish Ministers* 2014 S.C. 490; 2014 S.L.T. 335.

increasingly sophisticated principles designed to determine when they should and should not interfere. One such distinction is between policy and operational decisions, as to which the courts operate an assumption that in the formation of policy the Executive is intended to have very broad discretion with which the courts will hesitate to interfere, while in relation to operational matters it is reasonable for the courts to exercise a relatively tight degree of control and supervision.[98a]

Duty to exercise powers for intended purpose

[New paragraph] **12.4.13**

However broad the terms in which a power is conferred, Ministers are under a duty to search for and give effect to the legislative intent in conferring it:

> "99. It is a general principle of administrative law that a public body must exercise a statutory power for the purpose for which the power was conferred by Parliament, and not for any unauthorised purpose. An unauthorised purpose may be laudable in its own right, yet still unlawful. The issue is not whether or not the public body has acted in the public interest, but whether it has acted in accordance with the purpose for which the statutory power was conferred."[98b]

[98a] "Not all decisions by public authorities involve questions of policy and the courts have evolved a distinction between "operational" decisions on the one hand and "policy" decisions on the other. The courts generally will not impose a duty of care in respect of policy decisions but will do so in respect of operational decisions. The drawing of the boundary between the two will sometimes be difficult. In general terms the greater the element of policy involved the wider the area of discretion accorded by the courts to the public authority and the more likely it is that the matter is not justiciable: Lord Slynn of Hadley in Barrett at page 571G.

[69] In drawing the line it is however important to understand the rationale for the court's self restraint in respect of policy decisions. As Lord Hutton summarised the position in Barrett (at page 583C)

'It is only where the decision involves the weighing of competing public interests or is dictated by considerations which the courts are not fitted to assess that the courts will hold that the issue is non justiciable on the ground that the decision was made in exercise of a statutory discretion.'

[70] Lord Hutton then goes on to quote with approval the judgment of Mason J. in Sutherland Shire Council at page 468 to 469:

'The distinction between policy and operational factors is not easy to formulate but the dividing line between them will be observed if we recognise that the public authority is under no duty of care in relation to decisions which involve or are dictated by financial, economic, social or political factors or restraints.' "—*Santander UK Plc v Keeper of the Registers of Scotland* [2013] ScotCS CSOH 24.

[98b] *R. (on the application of Core Issues Trust Ltd) v Transport for London* [2014] EWHC 2628 (Admin); see also *R. (on the application of Attfield) v Barnet LBC* [2013] EWHC 2089 (Admin); see also—"19. Article 4(3) of the 2013 Order provides on its face that the effect of a certificate under section 2C(1)(c) of the 1997 Act in respect of an exclusion direction made before 25 June 2013 is automatically to terminate any existing judicial review proceedings which relate to that direction. If that is indeed the legal effect of such a certificate, it is a truly remarkable result, since it puts in the hands of the Secretary of State, as a party to (indeed, a defendant to) judicial review proceedings, the power to bring about the termination of those proceedings by her own act and without any intervention by the court; and to do so irrespective of the stage that the proceedings have reached,

SECTION 6

ENFORCEMENT

Mandatory or directory?

12.6.4.A1 *[New paragraph—insert before heading for 12.6.4.1]*

The distinction between mandatory and directory duties has never been considered completely satisfactory. An alternative has been suggested as follows:

> "The Notice failed to comply with section 13(3)(e) of the 1993 Act because it did not give the names of one of the qualifying tenants in the Property, the address of the flat of that qualifying tenant and the particulars of that qualifying tenant's lease as specified in section 13(3)(e)(i). ... Where a statute lays down a process or procedure for the exercise or acquisition by a person or body of some right conferred by the statute, and the statute does not expressly state what is the consequence of the failure to comply with that process or procedure, the consequence used to be said to depend on whether the requirement was mandatory or directory. If, on the proper interpretation of the statute, it was held to be mandatory, the failure to comply was said to invalidate everything which followed. If it was held, on the proper interpretation of the statute, to be directory, the failure to comply would not necessarily have invalidated what followed.
>
> That approach is now regarded as unsatisfactory since the characterisation of the statutory provisions as either mandatory or directory really does no more than state a conclusion as to the consequence of non-compliance rather than assist in determining what consequence the legislature intended. The modern approach is to determine the consequence of non-compliance as an ordinary issue of statutory interpretation, applying all the usual principles of statutory interpretation. It invariably involves, therefore, among other things according to the context, an assessment of the purpose and importance of the requirement in the context of the statutory scheme as a whole."[141a]

---

whether at first instance or on appeal. Mr Phillips accepted in argument that such a provision would be 'most unusual'—he could not point to any equivalent—and that very clear language was required to show that this was Parliament's intention. But he submitted that the statutory language was clear and that Parliament can be seen to have intended this result. ... It follows that in purporting to provide, by article 4(3) of the 2013 Order, that a certificate under section 2C(1)(c) of the 1997 Act in relation to a direction made before the commencement day 'terminates any judicial review proceedings, or proceedings on appeal from such proceedings', the Secretary of State was acting outside the powers conferred on her by the 2013 Act. ... 34. For the reasons given I would allow the appeal, declare that article 4(3) of the 2013 Order is outside the powers conferred by the 2013 Act and that the judicial review proceedings relating to the exclusion direction have not been terminated by the making of the certificate, and remit the case to the Administrative Court to decide on the future of those proceedings." —*R. (on the application of Ignaoua) v Secretary of State for the Home Department* [2013] EWCA Civ 1498.

[141a] *Natt v Osman* [2014] EWCA Civ 1520.

Interaction with criminal law

[New paragraph] **12.6.14.1**

(For discussion of the interaction between criminal and civil remedies see para.1.6.17.)

Chapter 13

STATUTORY CORPORATIONS

Constraints on action

[Insert at end of note 7]   **13.1.2**

; see also—"44. Two relevant principles of statutory interpretation were not in dispute between the parties, and are uncontroversial. First, a public body created by statute can only do that which it is authorised to do by positive law (see, e.g., *R v Secretary of State for Health ex parte B* [1999] 1 F.L.R. 656 per Scott Baker LJ at 668G). Second, statutory provisions should be interpreted in accordance with the purpose and intention of Parliament as expressed in the words they used."—*R. (on the application of Welsh Language Commissioner) v National Savings and Investments* [2014] EWHC 488 (Admin).

CHAPTER 14

EFFECT ON OTHER LAW

SECTION 1

EFFECT ON COMMON LAW

Increasing judicial reluctance to make new law

[Add new paragraphs to end of 14.1.5.1]   **14.1.5.1**

In essence the courts' reluctance to become involved in the development of legislation can be summarised as a reluctance to being used by citizens to achieve legislative change which they could, and therefore should as a matter of democratic principle, achieve through Parliament.[26a]

There is also a reluctance to assume that Parliament necessarily intended to achieve the fullest or most extreme effects of the stated policy underlying the legislation.[26b]

[26a] See, for example of the articulation of the principle involved: "81. In my judgment, where delegated legislation is challenged on the ground that it thwarts or frustrates the statutory purpose, it is permissible for the Court to be informed of the extent of Parliament's knowledge and approval of the provisions under challenge when enacting the enabling legislation. Otherwise the Court may proceed on a false assumption or be misled. Although the Court may conclude that delegated legislation is ultra vires, despite approval by Parliament, it must decline to intervene where, in effect, a claimant asks it to enter the political arena and substitute its views for those of Parliament. In my view, that is what the Claimant invites the Court to do in this case. As Lord Bingham explained in *R (Countryside Alliance & Ors) v Attorney General & Ors* [2008] 1 A.C. 719 (a human rights challenge to the hunting ban) at [45], '[t]he democratic process is liable to be subverted, if on a question of moral and political judgment, opponents of the Act achieve through the courts that which they could not achieve in Parliament'."—*R. (on the application of Rights of Women) v Lord Chancellor and Secretary of State for Justice* [2015] EWHC 35 (Admin).

[26b] "170. It is a common place in legislation that objectives may not be fully achievable or achieved. Compromises or concessions have to be made if legislators are to achieve the enactment of particular provisions. This is perhaps especially so at the international European level, in the case of measures agreed by the Council of Ministers where different Member States may only have been prepared to go part of the way with a Commission proposal (or Parliamentary proposal for amendment) and qualifications may have to be introduced to arrive at any agreement. The structure of the European Union involves a balance of interests which must be respected if the structure is to be stable. 171. When reading or interpreting legislation, it can never therefore be assumed that particular objectives have been achieved to the fullest possible degree. Limitations on the scope or application of a legislative measure may have been necessary to achieve agreement. There may also

Clear conflict between common law and legislation

14.1.10.A1   *[New paragraph]*

The relationship between prerogative powers and legislation has been sum-marised as follows:

> "The exercise of a prerogative power may however be suspended, or abrogated, by an Act of Parliament: *Attorney-General v De Keyser's Royal Hotel* [1920] A.C. 508, per Lord Atkinson at pp 539–540. So a statute which operates in the field of prerogative may exclude the possibility of exercising prerogative powers. Where a complete and exhaustive code is to be found in the statute, any powers under the prerogative which would otherwise have applied are excluded entirely: see, eg, *Re Mitchell* [1954] Ch 525. Any exercise of a prerogative power in a manner, or for a purpose, which is inconsistent with the statute will be an abuse of power: *R v Secretary of State for the Home Department, Ex p Fire Brigades Union* [1995] 2 AC 513, per Lord Nicholls of Birkenhead at p 576."[56a]

SECTION 3

AMENDMENT OF EARLIER LEGISLATION

Speaking amendments

14.3.5   *[Insert new note 118a at end of paragraph]*

[118a] "I take the view that one can apply the "always speaking" approach to statutory construction to the provisions of the Schedule to the CFO, although we are not called upon on this appeal to express any view as to whether, so interpreted, they were satisfied by airlines other than Ryanair in the period under review. But I am also satisfied that, whether or not they can be so interpreted, the correct approach to construction is not to delete Notes (5)(b) and (6) from the Schedule. Lord Pannick's point that some support for Ryanair's construction can be derived from the present impossibility of literal compliance with the conjunction tickets provisions is, I think, misplaced. The CFO cannot be construed by reference to subsequent events which were not necessarily foreseeable in 1994 and, when looked at in the context of the ticketing practices at that time, its provisions were entirely workable."—*Ryanair Ltd v HM Revenue and Customs* [2014] EWCA Civ 410.

have been good reasons for limitations, of which courts are unaware or are not the best judge. Where the legislature has agreed a clearly expressed measure, reflecting the legislators' choices and compromises in order to achieve agreement, it is not for courts to rewrite the legislation, to extend or 'improve' it in respects which the legislator clearly did not intend."—*R. (on the application of HS2 Action Alliance Ltd) v Secretary of State for Transport* [2014] UKSC 3.

[56a] *R. (on the application of Alvi) v Secretary of State for the Home Department* [2012] UKSC 33.

CHAPTER 15

ERRORS IN LEGISLATION

Beneficial construction to repair obvious error

[Insert at end of note 18]   **15.1.7.1**

; see also: "10. Under the interpretative approach in *Inco Europe*, a court may be permitted in certain very limited circumstances to adopt an interpretation of a legislative provision which has the practical effect of rectifying a defect in its drafting. In this case, the Secretary of State maintains that the circumstances surrounding the promulgation of the Commencement Order are such that it is appropriate for the relevant part of it to be interpreted so as to cover the immigration control zones in France as well as United Kingdom territory, pursuant to the guidance in *Inco Europe*. Mr Eadie QC, for the Secretary of State, submits that this means that the Commencement Order was effective to bring the amendments to the 1999 Act under the 2002 Act into force in relation to clandestine entrants found in a vehicle in an immigration control zone in France. 11. Mr Nicholls QC, as Advocate to the Court, presents the opposing argument. He submits that the Commencement Order cannot properly be given such a rectified interpretation by the court. He says that this means that there was no lawful basis for the civil penalties to be imposed in this case. ... 34. On a literal reading, the Commencement Order only brought the 2002 Act amendments of Part II of the 1999 Act into force in relation to clandestine entrants arriving on United Kingdom territory concealed in a vehicle or rail freight wagon. But should a rectifying interpretation be given to the Commencement Order, on the basis of the principle in Inco Europe, so that it has effect to bring those amendments into force in relation to clandestine entrants arriving in a prescribed immigration control zone as well? ... 52. I turn, then, to consider the application of these principles of legislative interpretation in relation to Part II of the 1999 Act and the Commencement Order. In my judgment, this is a case in that exceptional class in which it is appropriate to imply wording into the relevant legislative provision, by application of the approach in Inco Europe, notwithstanding the penal context in which the exercise of interpretation falls to be carried out. I consider that, on its true construction, the relevant text in the Commencement Order is to be read as including by clear implication additional wording to indicate that the 2002 Act amendments also apply in relation to immigration control zones."—*Bogdanic v The Secretary of State for the Home Department* [2014] EWHC 2872 (QB).

15.1.7.1 *[Insert at end of first paragraph]*

But the courts are resistant to attempts to turn this into anything like a rigid rule against the correction of mistakes in penal contexts or to be too readily persuaded that a context is penal for these purposes.[18a]

Status of *Inco* rule

15.1.7.2 *[New paragraph]*

The courts have been careful to point out that the rule in *Inco* is not about permitting a degree of judicial law-making in the face of a legislative error; it is simply a case of a rule of statutory interpretation required to be applied in specific situations, similar to the presumption against absurdity and other legislative canons.[22a]

[18a] See, for example: "43. The present case, the claimants submitted, involves penal legislation, and for that reason the court should not correct a mistake, even if the conditions are met. On this point, I agree with the Environment Agency. These provisions are only penal in the sense that intentional obstruction of authorised persons in the exercise of their powers is an offence (I have set out the provisions of s.110 Environment Act 1995 above). I do not consider that this should inhibit the court from making a correction if the strict requirements as laid down in the *Inco* case are otherwise met. *R v C* [2008] 1 Cr. App. R. 22, and *R (SSHD) v Southwark Crown Court* [2013] EWHC 4366 is authority which supports that approach. . . . The above gives a sensible construction to the provisions read as a whole, and in my respectful view this reading can be reached as a matter of construction. In the alternative, I would conclude that the court can be 'abundantly sure' of the three matters set out in the passage from the *Inco* case set out above, and the provision interpreted by reading words into the section. As to the substance of the provision Parliament would have made had the error in the Bill been noticed (explained in *Inco* to be a matter of crucial importance), as it was put in *Pollen Estate Trustee Co Ltd v Revenue and Customs Commissioners* [2013] 1 W.L.R. 3785 [49] (Lewison LJ), 'We are not parliamentary draftsmen; and it is sufficient that we can be confident of the gist or substance of the alteration, rather than its precise language'. In my view, the gist or substance is as set out above."—*Allensway Recycling Ltd v The Environment Agency* [2014] EWHC 1638 (Admin).

[22a] See, for example: "41. It is important to emphasise that *Inco Europe* states a principle of interpretation of a legislative instrument. Effect is to be given to the intention of the legislator, as expressed in the instrument as objectively construed in accordance with the principles identified in cases such as *Black-Clawson International and Fothergill*, supra, and *R v Secretary of State for the Environment, Transport and the Regions, ex p. Spath Holme Ltd* [2001] 2 A.C. 349, especially at 396F-399E per Lord Nicholls. As Lord Nicholls there observed (at 397G), although it is legitimate to have regard to certain aids to interpretation of legislation which are external to the legislation itself, 'This gives rise to a tension between the need for legal certainty, which is one of the fundamental elements of the rule of law, and the need to give effect to the intention of Parliament, from whatever source that (objectively assessed) intention can be gleaned.' 42. For the purposes of the principle in Inco Europe, it is only if the legislative instrument has a clear, objectively assessed meaning, having regard to all the circumstances and all indicators of the legislator's intention available to the person subject to the law (assisted as necessary by his legal advisers), and that meaning is contrary to the literal meaning of the text of the instrument, that it will be appropriate for the Court to give a rectifying interpretation to the instrument. Given the primacy ordinarily to be given to the language used in a legislative instrument as an indicator of the legislator's intention, the countervailing objective indicators that, despite the language used, the legislator's intention was different need to be very strong, as Lord Nicholls emphasised in *Inco Europe*. It must be clear that the true intention of the legislator, objectively assessed, was different from the language used by the draftsman. It is only if the Court has no doubt that the draftsman 'slipped up' (see *Inco Europe* at p. 592A), i.e. that there was a mistake made in the language chosen by the draftsman to give effect to the intention of the

For an interesting case where European Union law, human rights and Inco merged together see *Jessemey v Rowstock Ltd.*[22b]

Increasing incidence of mistakes in Acts

[New paragraph]   **15.1.10**

There is certainly a judicial perception that *Inco* has been applied or considered in an increasing number of cases in recent years.[25] It is, of course, an open question whether this reflects a drop in the quality of legislative drafting or an increased judicial willingness to be assertive in correcting it. What is clear, however, is that the courts do not feel constrained to apply the *Inco* rules only in relation to modern legislation and, to that extent at least, in so far as there is a trend towards increased reliance on the rules one might suggest that it says more about modern judicial attitudes than about modern legislation.[26] It is, however, of course possible that a deterioration in legislative quality has led the courts to

---

legislator, that it can be confident that the proper interpretation of the provision is given by other objective indicators of the legislator's intention. This is an approach to interpretation of a kind which is not unique to legislative instruments, but is of general application in the construction of all sorts of instruments which are intended to have legal effects: compare, e.g., *Mannai Investment Co. Ltd v Eagle Star Life Assurance Co. Ltd* [1997] A.C. 749, esp. at 797G per Lord Steyn. 43. Although in this judgment I have used the expression 'rectifying interpretation' as a convenient shorthand expression for the process of construction pursuant to the guidance in Inco Europe, I should make clear that properly speaking the court does not rectify or amend the legislative instrument. It gives it its true meaning, arrived at by the process of objective interpretation described in the authorities referred to above."—*Bogdanic v The Secretary of State for the Home Department* [2014] EWHC 2872 (QB).

[22b] [2014] EWCA Civ 185.

[25] "51. It is not necessary to go back to cases decided before Inco Europe. As it happens, since that decision, there appear to have been an increasing number of cases in which the principles in Inco Europe have been discussed. Counsel have referred me to a large number of such cases. However, it was not suggested that any of the later cases have changed in any way the principles helpfully identified in Inco Europe, although counsel for the Second Defendant suggested that one later case provided a gloss, and possibly a limitation, on those principles. In another later case, *Director of the Serious Fraud Office v B (No. 2)* [2012] 1 W.L.R. 3188, Gross LJ at [21] said, having cited Inco Europe:

'Further citation of authority is unnecessary in this regard. The principles set out by Lord Nicholls have been considered in a number of subsequent decisions; unsurprisingly, rectification was possible in some cases but not in others, depending on the individual facts. It may be noted that the question of the standard of proof (i.e. that the court should be "abundantly sure" that the threshold conditions were met) was real, important and, in some cases, decisive.'

52. I agree (with respect) with Gross LJ's comment in *Director of the Serious Fraud Office v B (No. 2)* as to the need to cite further authority. However, out of deference to the detailed submissions of counsel who cited many cases which discussed Inco Europe I will mention some, but not all, of the cases cited to me. Further, even if those cases do not change the legal principles summarised in Inco Europe, it may be helpful in the present case to refer to those decisions which provide useful illustrations of how these principles have been applied."—*Industry-Wide Coal Staff Superannuation Scheme Co-Ordinator Ltd v Industry-Wide Coal Staff Superannuation Scheme Trustees Ltd* [2012] EWHC 3712 (Ch).

[26] For an illustrative case of the application of Inco resulting in judicial rectification of the Administration of Justice Act 1960 s.13 see *OB v Serious Fraud Office* [2012] EWCA Civ 501; *OB v The Director of the Serious Fraud Office* [2012] EWCA Crim 901.

reconsider their deference to it, and that the results have then been extended backwards in time towards older legislation.

15.1.11 *[New paragraph]*

On some occasions, it will be less than clear whether the court is correcting an error in drafting under the rule in *Inco* or adopting a beneficial construction in accordance with the presumption against absurdity. The approach of the court will sometimes stress only the substantive result to be achieved, without thinking it necessary to be too specific about the mechanism being adopted in order to achieve it.[27] In other cases, it will be clear that the court is applying the rules for the correction of drafting mistakes, without it being thought necessary to cite *Inco* expressly.[28]

15.1.12 *[New paragraph]*

The Political and Constitutional Reform Select Committee of the House of Commons' Report *Ensuring standards in the quality of legislation*[29] notes the increasing application of the rules in *Inco* in the following terms[30]:

> "We were told that judges were making increasing use of the "Inco rule" which allows Courts to correct obvious drafting errors by, in suitable cases, adding, omitting or substituting words to discharge the Court's interpretive function. . . .
>
> 50. The recent judgment in *R (Noone) v The Governor of HMP Drake Hall*[54] provides an example of a case where poor quality legislation resulted in what should have been a simple question necessitating an appeal to the Supreme Court. The case concerned the interrelationship between the sentencing provisions of the Criminal Justice Act 1991 and the Criminal Justice Act 2003 for prisoners serving consecutive sentences of above and below 12 months. The Court was attempting to work out the date on which the Appellant became eligible to be considered for a home detention curfew.

---

[27] See, for example: "In my judgment the 'duties' referred to in section 189 are therefore those statutory duties under the 1974 Act which the assignee has to perform in order to enforce his assigned rights. These duties have 'passed by assignment' in the sense that it is by reason of the assignment that the assignee becomes obliged to fulfil them. It is not necessary to add to or change the language of section 189 in order to interpret it in the manner suggested. Even if it was, there would be no difficulty in so doing in order to avoid the obviously absurd consequence of rights under a credit agreement not being effectively assignable. That could be done, as has been suggested, by interpreting 'rights and duties' as meaning 'rights and/or duties'. The section applies to both transfers of rights (by assignment or operation of law) and to transfers of rights and duties (by operation of law) as the case may be."—*Jones v Link Financial Ltd* [2012] EWHC 2402 (QB).

[28] For a case in which the court considered the extent of permissible correction of errors in secondary legislation without reference to *Inco*, see *ITAU BBA International Ltd, Re* [2012] EWHC 1783 (Ch).

[29] May 20, 2013; HC 85.

[30] pp.15–16.

The answer was dependent upon which of the two schemes contained in the two Acts applied, or whether a third scheme pursuant to the transitional provisions applicable between the two Acts applied.

51. The Supreme Court held that an interpretation of the transitional provisions had "wholly implausible and unacceptable consequences". Lord Judge commented: 'Ill considered commencement and transitional provisions, which have to negotiate their way around and through legislation which has been enacted but which for one reason or another has not or will not be brought into force, add to the burdens. [. . .]The explanation for the problem is simple. For too many years now the administration of criminal justice has been engulfed by a relentless tidal wave of legislation. The tide is always in flow: it has never ebbed. [. . .] It is outrageous that so much intellectual effort, as well as public time and resources, have had to be expended in order to discover a route through the legislative morass to what should be, both for the prisoner herself, and for those responsible for her custody, the prison authorities, the simplest and most certain of questions—the prisoner's release date.'

52. This case is a clear example of bad quality legislation requiring time and money to be expended to rectify problems which could and should have been identified during the preparation of the policy or at the very least rectified during the Bill's passage through Parliament."

[New paragraph]   **15.1.13**

The Committee's Report magnanimously concludes that "the majority of poor quality legislation results from either inadequate policy preparation or insufficient time being allowed for the drafting process, or a combination of the two. This is not to point the finger at the Office of the Parliamentary Counsel, which neither produces policy nor determines the speed with which policy is to be transformed into legislative proposals."

[New paragraph]   **15.1.14**

Generous-spirited though this is, it may be that one of the reasons why a number of fundamental problems in relation to legislation are no nearer tolerable solution now than they were at the time of the Renton Report 40 years ago is the tendency to ascribe the difficulties to "circumstances" rather than to attribute responsibility to particular offices and even individuals. If Parliamentary Counsel are not responsible for the judicial perception that the quality of primary legislation is deteriorating, then it is difficult to know who is responsible or who else could be expected to do anything about it.

[New paragraph]   **15.1.15**

One of the *Inco* conditions was originally that the court should be able to be certain not just as to the policy that was intended to be enacted but also as to the precise terms that should have been employed to achieve it; but there are signs that the as the pace of judicial resolution increases not to allow drafting deficiency to defeat clear legislative intention, they are less willing to be deterred by semantic uncertainties around the precise language that could or should have been used, provided the policy is clear.[31]

---

[31] See, for example: "The reading of paragraph 1 (1) [of Finance Act 2003 Schedule 8] which I would favour is: 'A land transaction is exempt from charge [to the extent that] the purchaser is a charity and the following conditions are met.' 48. Thus exemption would be available to the extent that the purchaser is a charity and to the extent that the conditions are met. This reading would have the consequence that a land transaction is partially exempt, but only to the extent of a charity's interest. Ms Tipples objected that this reading did not work because the condition in paragraph 1 (2) could not be satisfied. The argument was that because the 'purchaser' was not the charity alone, it could not be said that the 'purchaser' would hold 'the subject-matter of the transaction' for qualifying charitable purposes. But the essence of HMRC's case (which I have accepted) is that the beneficial owners of the property in question (here the equitable estate in fee simple) must be viewed collectively. Viewed collectively, I cannot see why it is impossible to determine the extent to which, collectively, they hold the equitable estate for qualifying charitable purposes. Ms Tipples then submitted that the reading I favour goes too far, because it would have the result that the whole transaction would escape SDLT. But I do not consider that that is correct. If the exemption is afforded 'to the extent that' the conditions are met, this concern evaporates. The third objection is that there is no machinery for determining what part of the interest is held for qualifying charitable purposes. But under Schedule 8 para 3 a charity is entitled to relief if it holds the 'greater part' of the subject-matter of the transaction for qualifying charitable purposes. There is no machinery for determining whether that condition is satisfied, so the absence of machinery cannot be an insuperable objection. Moreover, there is no indication in paragraph 3 whether the 'greater part' is greater by area or greater in value. **Uncertainty at the edges cannot be decisive either.** 49. Despite Ms Tipples' objections it seems to me there is a sufficient 'policy imperative' to justify the reading I favour. I believe that it is also consonant with the approach of Lord Nicholls in *Inco Europe*. **We are not Parliamentary draftsmen; and it is sufficient that we can be confident of the gist or substance of the alteration, rather than its precise language. In substance what this means is that the exemption would apply as regards that proportion of the beneficial interest that is attributable to the undivided share held by the charity for qualifying charitable purposes. I do not see that this gives rise to any conceptual uncertainty or to any insuperable practical administrative problems.** In my judgment this reading is necessary in order to give effect to what must have been Parliament's intention as regards the taxation of charities. There has been no principled reason advanced why a charity should be exempt from SDLT in the situations to which I have referred in [19]; but not be entitled to any relief at all on its proportionate undivided share in a jointly acquired property. Not to afford a charity relief in such circumstances would, in my judgment, be capricious."—*The Pollen Estate Trustee Company Ltd v Revenue and Customs Commissioners* [2013] EWCA Civ 753 (editor's emphasis).

Chapter 16

INTRODUCTION TO STATUTORY INTERPRETATION

Authority for construction of legislation

[Amendment]   **16.1.7**

This paragraph should now be read with references to the higher courts, as established by the Senior Courts Act 1981 (as it has now been renamed) and headed by the Supreme Court. The reference to the House of Lords is now obsolete.

CHAPTER 18

LITERAL OR PURPOSIVE INTERPRETATION

Introduction

[Insert at end of note 2]   **18.1.1**

; see also: "Nor, as noted by *Craies*, is a simplistic bifurcation of approach between supposedly literal and purposive schools of interpretation likely to assist. What is essential is to consider the disputed text in context of the terms of the Regulations as a whole, the scheme of the Regulations and the terms of the 1995 Act, taking account of the terms of the new amending regulations and of other decisions on the disputed text."—*Scottish Legal Aid Board v Lavery Sheriff Court (Glasgow and Strathkelvin) (Glasgow)*, January 7, 2015.

Contextual construction

[New Paragraph]   **18.1.7.2**

A concentration on context must not be allowed to become an excuse for reading the words properly and giving them their natural language meaning.[31a]

Limitation of purposive construction: danger of speculating on legislative intent

[Insert at end of note 37]   **18.1.9**

; see also, "In my opinion the 'purposive' interpretation put forward by counsel for the interested party completely distorts the plain language of the statutory provisions. In order to give effect to it, I think it would be necessary to rewrite

---

[31a] See, for example: "10. I accept that it is easy, when seeking to construe a statutory expression in its proper context, to overlook the impact of the particular expression or words used by the draughtsman. 'If the terms of the definition are ambiguous, the choice of the term to be defined may throw some light on what they mean' (Lord Hoffmann in *Macdonald v Dextra Accessories Limited* [2005] A.C. 1111 [18]). 11. But there is no ambiguity in the definition of 'banker's profits'. 'The value, in money or money's worth, of the stakes staked' means what it says: it is the value of the chips risked in the relevant charging period."—*Aspinalls Club Ltd v Revenue and Customs Commissioners* [2013] EWCA Civ 1464.

the terms of the statutory provisions. I appreciate that counsel for the interested party is concerned about the results of the respondents' interpretation. I agree with the concerns. Her construction is an attempt, in my opinion, to try to avoid these results. I consider however it is only necessary for her to do this because of the attempt to interpret section 36 in the context of Part 1 of this Act as permitting any person to apply for consent for construction and operation even if they are not a licence holder or a person authorised by an exemption to generate. On the construction put forward by the petitioners, there is nothing odd or absurd about the results of the interpretation of Schedule 9 and section 36 in the context of Part 1 of this Act."—*Sustainable Shetland v Scottish Ministers* [2013] CSOH 158; 2013 S.L.T. 1173.

Fiscal statutes

18.1.13.5.1 *[New paragraph]*

See also the following extract from the judgment in *Aberdeen Asset Management Plc v HM Revenue and Customs*[57a]—

"This question must be considered in the light of the line of authority that has followed the decision in *WT Ramsay Ltd v IRC* [1982] A.C. 300; 54 TC 101; [1981] STC 174. Two fundamental principles emerge from those cases. First, revenue statutes should be interpreted in accordance with the normal principles of statutory interpretation; the court is not confined to a literal interpretation, and the words used in the statute should be considered in the context of the relevant statutory provisions taken as a whole, including the purpose of those provisions. Secondly, the court must ascertain the legal nature of any transaction to which it is sought to attach tax consequences, and if that involves considering a series of transactions, it is the whole series that must be considered. Perhaps the most helpful statements of the law are now found in *Barclays Mercantile Business Finance Ltd v Mawson* [2005] STC 1; [2004] UKHL 51, where the effect of the previous case law is summarized. First, at paragraphs [32]–[33] Lord Nicholls stated:

'The essence of the new approach was to give the statutory provision purposive construction in order to determine the nature of the transaction to which it was intended to apply and then to decide whether the actual transaction (which might involve considering the overall effect of a number of elements intended to operate together) answered to the statutory description. Of course this does not mean that the courts have to put their reasoning into the straitjacket of first construing the statute in the abstract and then looking at the facts. It might be more convenient to analyse the facts and then ask whether they satisfy the requirements of the

---

[57a] [2013] CSIH 84; 2014 S.C. 271.

statute. But however one approaches the matter, the question is always whether the relevant provision of statute, upon its true construction, applies to the facts as found . . . .

The simplicity of this question, however difficult it might be to answer on the facts of a particular case, shows that the *Ramsay* case did not introduce a new doctrine operating within the special field of revenue statutes'.

Then, at paragraph [36], it is stated:

'[Previous cases] gave rise to a view that, in the application of any taxing statute, transactions or elements of transactions which had no commercial purpose were to be disregarded. But that is going too far. It elides the two steps which are necessary in the application of any statutory provision: first, to decide, on a purposive construction, exactly what transaction will answer to the statutory description and secondly, to decide whether the transaction in question does so. As Ribeiro PJ said in Collector of *Stamp Revenue v Arrowtown Assets Ltd* [2003] HKCFA 46 at [35] . . . :

'[T]he driving principle in the Ramsay line of cases continues to involve a general rule of statutory construction and an unblinking approach to the analysis of the facts. The ultimate question is whether the relevant statutory provisions, construed purposively, were intended to apply to the transaction, viewed realistically'.

Emphasis was also placed on the need to focus carefully upon the particular statutory provision and to identify its requirements before one can decide whether circular payments or elements inserted for the purpose of tax avoidance should be disregarded or treated as irrelevant for the purposes of the statute: see paragraph [38]."—*Aberdeen Asset Management Plc v HM Revenue and Customs* [2013] CSIH 84; 2014 S.C. 271.

Non-legislative interpretation: commercial documents

[Insert at end of note 67]   **18.1.13.7.1**

; see also—"14. The principles for interpreting patents have been subject to considerable judicial analysis and refinement over time and are now well established. Although they share many of the same elements as the principles of interpretation in other areas of law, they have the special feature of being subject to the overarching provisions of section 125 of the Patents Act 1977, which itself is intended to give effect to Article 69 of the European Patent Convention ('the EPC') and its Protocol."—*Microsoft Corporation v Motorola Mobility LLC* [2013] EWCA Civ 1613.

CHAPTER 19

REBUTTABLE PRESUMPTIONS OF CONSTRUCTION

Presumption against unfairness

[New paragraph]   **19.1.5.1**

The presumption of fairness affects all aspects of the interpretation and application of statutory functions.[12a]

Presumption against double jeopardy

[New paragraph]   **19.1.7.2**

In so far as part of the concept of double jeopardy concerns giving multiple consequences to a single event or series of events, it can be difficult to determine what amounts to a single event or series of events for that purpose.[22a]

[12a] "[32] 'There is a general presumption that the legislature does not intend to achieve a result that is manifestly unfair, unreasonable or arbitrary': see 19.1.5 of *Craies on Legislation*. Lord Diplock made clear the presumption extends to the nature of the powers and duties conferred by statute. In *Hillingdon London Borough Council v Commission for Racial Equality* [1982] A.C. 779 at 787 he said: 'Where an Act of Parliament confers upon an administrative body functions which involve its making decisions which affect to their detriment the rights of other persons or curtail their liberty to do as they please, there is a presumption that Parliament intended that the administrative body should act fairly towards those persons who will be affected by their decisions'."—*Swann's Application for Judicial Review, Re* [2014] NIQB 81; see also—"91. Lord Browne-Wilkinson described this as a principle of construction requiring the courts to interpret even very wide words in a statute as implicitly limited by the presumption that Parliament intends the Common Law requirements of fairness to apply unless it has indicated to the contrary (*Pierson v Secretary of State for the Home Department* [1998] A.C. 539, 573–4). Parliament does not legislate in a vacuum: statutes are drafted on the basis that the ordinary rules and principles of the Common Law will apply to the express statutory provisions (ibid, at 573–4). The duty of fairness governing the exercise of a statutory power is a limitation on the discretion of the decision-maker which is implied into the statute (*Bank Mellat (Appellant) v Her Majesty's Treasury (Respondent) (No. 2)* [2013] UKSC 39, per Lord Sumption at paragraph [35])."—*R. (on the application of Plantagenet Alliance Ltd) v Secretary of State for Justice* [2014] EWHC 1662 (QB).

[22a] See, for example: "It is clear that different evidence from witnesses will be required to prove the US offences, and that the victims named in the US indictment are entirely different from those in the UK indictment without overlap in the harm caused or losses suffered. In those circumstances I do not consider that the US proceedings can be described as founded on the same or substantially the same facts as the UK proceedings. There was no obligation on the UK authorities to prosecute in relation to offences which might involve American victims, and no evidence was put before the court with a view to proving those offences."—*Kulibaba v Government of the United States of America* [2014] EWHC 176 (Admin).

(For discussion of the interaction between criminal and civil remedies see para.1.6.17.)

Presumption against expropriation

19.1.8   *[Add to note 25]*

For an example of the application of this presumption, see: "Further, section 24D(2) is to be read in light of the usual presumption that Parliament does not intend to interfere with property rights without compensation: see e.g. *Westminster Bank Ltd v Beverley Borough Council* [1971] A.C. 508, 529 (per Lord Reid); *Maxwell on the Interpretation of Statutes*, 12th ed., pp. 251–262 (esp. p. 253: 'A . . . restrictive construction is placed on statutes which interfere with rights of property'). If the relevant phrase in section 24D(1) were not interpreted with the restrictive sense which I prefer, I consider it would infringe this presumption, since it would deprive the tenant of the fruits or incidents of his rights in relation to his own property by requiring him to pay rent for what is properly to be regarded as his own. Since there is an alternative, sensible construction of the phrase which avoids this result, that construction is to be preferred."—*Humber Oil Terminals Trustee Ltd (HOTT) v Associated British Ports (ABP)* [2012] EWHC 1336 (Ch).

[Add after the second sub-paragraph (ending " . . . exhibited by the deprivation or interference.")]

The essence of the presumption against expropriation is that the courts lean against a construction of public general legislation which interferes with private rights, and presumes that as little interference was intended as is consistent with the clear policy intention of the Act. That being so, it can sometimes be the case that the construction which interferes least as against one set of private interests is the most detrimental to another; in which case the legislative intent may have to be determined without the benefit of simply relying on the presumption against expropriation, which might produce an arbitrary result in favour of one class of interests as against the other.[25a]

[25a] "Although the 1967 Act like the 1993 Act is in a sense expropriatory, in that it confers rights on lessees to acquire rights compulsorily from their lessors, this has been held not to give rise to any interpretative presumption in favour of the latter. As Millett LJ said of the 1993 Act: 'It would, in my opinion, be wrong to disregard the fact that, while the Act may to some extent be regarded as expropriatory of the landlord's interest, nevertheless it was passed for the benefit of tenants. It is the duty of the court to construe the 1993 Act fairly and with a view, if possible, to making it effective to confer on tenants those advantages which Parliament must have intended them to enjoy.' (*Cadogan v McGirk* [1996] 4 All E.R. 643, 648). By the same token, the court should avoid as far as possible an interpretation which has the effect of conferring rights going beyond those which Parliament intended."—*Day v Hosebay Ltd* [2012] UKSC 41.

Presumption against absurdity

[New paragraph]   **19.1.12.2**

The rule against absurdity remains an important aid for judges when deciding in which of two equally grammatical directions to jump in reading a provision; however, the courts remain alert to avoid attempts to use the rule to lead them into substituting their judgment for that of the legislature, even where the legislature's judgment was demonstrably ignorant or deficient.[40a]

Where the courts detect inescapable absurdity, they will sometimes commend the unhappy victim of the statutory anomaly to the favour of the administrative authorities in the hope that they will be able to find a way of mitigating the undesirable results of the statute while preserving its accurate and inevitable application.[40b]

[40a] See, for example: "82. Mr Eadie says, however, that that interpretation results in an absurdity, in that it attributes to Parliament an intention to extend the Crown guarantee not just to members as at the date of vesting, but also to post-transfer members. I accept that that is a result that Lord Mackay and his advisers did not intend, and I expect the legislature would probably regard such an interpretation of the legislation as resulting in an absurdity. But how does the claimed absurdity arise? The legislation proceeded, according to what we were told, on the basis of a statement made by Lord Mackay to the House of Lords that (a) related to the irrelevant section 68, and (b) was apparently made in ignorance of the terms of what became section 60. A consideration of what became section 60 would or should have told Parliament that the legislation, according to the ordinary interpretation of its language, failed to confine the Crown guarantee as Lord Mackay had explained. Moreover, if Lord Mackay, his advisers and Parliament had given any thought to how the Scheme worked, they would have seen that even the guarantee Parliament intended to give would not, upon the termination of the Scheme, have accrued exclusively to the benefit of the pre-transfer members. That is because the Scheme was not sectionalised as between pre- and post-transfer members, so that any guarantee payments made on a termination shortfall would simply serve to increase the available fund applicable for the benefit of both pre- and post-transfer members. If Parliament had given proper consideration to what the Crown guarantee was intended to achieve, it would have required the Corporation to close the Scheme to new members, and BT to open a new scheme for such members. The guarantee could then have been given in respect of the closed fund. 83. The problem the Secretary of State faces is, therefore, the fruit of shortcomings on the part of the Government in relation to the legislation intended to effect the offered guarantee. The outcome was legislation that, upon its ordinary construction, results in the guarantee taking effect as a guarantee of any outstanding liability of BT that vested in it under section 60. I can identify no proper basis upon which the court can interpret the legislation so as to provide the Crown with an escape from the guarantee to which our legislators voted to subject it. That would not be to interpret section 60, it would be to re-write it."—*Secretary of State for Culture, Media And Sport v BT Pension Scheme Trustees Ltd* [2014] EWCA Civ 958.

[40b] See, for example: "23. It follows from the above that I dismiss the appeal, properly argued though it was. 24. I would add this. I cannot believe that Parliament ever had in mind the exceptional circumstances raised by the facts of this case. I have little doubt that most proper thinking and well briefed parliamentarians would have thought that, in circumstances where the Legal Services Commission wrongly and wrongfully refused to classify the criminal case against MCA's client as a VHCC, where there was a massive amount of unforeseen and unforeseeable work necessary to address incorrect CCTV compilations and late and wrongly withheld CCTV evidence, attributable to the Crown's failings in the prosecution of that case and where, as here, the litigator has on all counts behaved with propriety, professionalism and a disregard for its own financial interest, there should be an exception to the rigours of Schedule 2. I would therefore invite the Lord Chancellor, in these exceptional circumstances to consider ways of providing appropriate recompense to MCA, albeit possibly on an ex gratia basis."—*Atkins v The Lord Chancellor* [2014] EWHC 1387 (QB).

Presumption against penalty

19.1.14.1   *[New paragraph]*

An extension or by-product of the presumption against the imposition of a penalty is the principle that legislation that does, or may, impose a penalty, is to be construed strictly against the Crown.[43a]

Presumption against creating or removing judicial jurisdiction

19.1.20   *[Replace final sentence of note 65]*

The final form of the provision (which was an inserted section 103A in the Nationality, Immigration and Asylum Act 2002, which has since been repealed) was as follows: "(1) A party to an appeal under section 82 or 83 may apply to the appropriate court, on the grounds that the Tribunal made an error of law, for an order requiring the Tribunal to reconsider its decision on the appeal. (2) The appropriate court may make an order under subsection (1)—(a) only if it thinks that the Tribunal may have made an error of law, and (b) only once in relation to an appeal."

Presumption against creating or removing judicial jurisdiction

19.1.22.A1   *[New paragraph—insert before 19.1.22.1]*

The fact that the specific procedure for determinations introduced by Parlia-

---

[43a] See: "47. The principle that penal legislation is to be construed strictly is a long-standing one, of recognised constitutional importance: ... The rationale for this principle is that it is presumed within our constitutional system that the legislator intends that a person subject to a penal regime should have been given fair warning of the risks he might face of being made subject to a penalty. 48. But it is not an absolute principle. The overarching requirement is that a court should give effect to the intention of the legislator, as objectively determined having regard to all relevant indicators and aids to construction. The principle of strict interpretation of penal legislation is one among many indicators of the meaning to be given to a legislative provision. It is capable of being outweighed by other objective indications of legislative intention, albeit it is itself an indicator of great weight. ... If other objective indicators of legislative meaning and intent are sufficiently clear, and it is obvious to the requisite degree that the draftsman has made a slip in the language he has used, a person subject to a penal regime may be taken to have been given fair warning even though the interpretation adopted by the court involves some implication of terms in, or substitution for, the text of a relevant legislative provision. ... 50. In my view, bearing this qualification firmly in mind, it is possible and may in a suitable case be appropriate to adopt an *Inco Europe* amending interpretation of a legislative provision in the context of penal legislation. That is in accordance with basic principles of statutory interpretation, as referred to above; see also *R (Kelly) v Secretary of State for Justice* [2008] EWCA Civ 177; [2009] QB 204 at [27]–[28] per Laws LJ. It is also of note that the Court of Appeal in *R v D* [2011] EWCA Crim 2082; [2012] 1 All E.R. 1108, at [66], whilst rejecting an argument that an *Inco Europe* amending interpretation in relation to a provision creating a substantive criminal offence should be adopted in that case, nevertheless stated '... we cannot rule out the application of the principles in the *Inco Europe* case in relation to a substantive criminal offence ... '."—*Bogdanic v The Secretary of State for the Home Department* [2014] EWHC 2872 (QB); see also para.29.1.13.

ment is capable of creating anomalies is not in itself a reason for the courts to assume supervisory jurisdiction.[77a]

Presumption of continued consistent interpretation

[New paragraph]   **19.1.22.1.2**

For a helpful summary of the principles applying to the construction of ouster clauses see the following extract from the judgment in *R. (on the application of Ignaoua) v Secretary of State for the Home Department*[81a]—

"21. Several strands of legal principle were submitted to be relevant to the task of statutory interpretation at the centre of this case. The first is the court's aversion to ouster clauses. Perhaps the seminal statement is Lord Reid's in *Anisminic v Foreign Compensation Commission* [1969] 2 A.C. 147: ouster clauses must be construed strictly, meaning that 'if such a provision is reasonably capable of having two meanings, that meaning shall be taken which preserves the ordinary jurisdiction of the court': at 170 C–D. In *R (Cart) v Upper Tribunal* [2009] EWHC 3052 (Admin) ([2011] QB 120 (on appeal [2010] EWCA Civ 859; 2011 UKSC 28; [2012] 1 A.C. 663), Laws LJ canvassed the authorities and concluded that it could not be supposed that judicial review might be ousted by an implication, far less one contained in a formula which amounted in effect to a deeming provision: [32]. Laws LJ went on to state that under the rule of law legislation could not be interpreted authoritatively by Parliament or the Executive, for they would be acting as judge in their own cause. The role of interpreter of legislation had to be performed by the court as an impartial and independent body: [36]–[37].

[77a] "vii) In exercising its power to exercise supervisory (judicial review) jurisdiction in this field the High Court must be aware that Parliament has deliberately allocated primary responsibility for determining disputes surrounding immigration and asylum decisions to the Tribunal system and that it would therefore run counter to the will of Parliament for the High Court routinely to assume to itself disputes about matters falling, prima facie, within the appellate Tribunal structure (Lim; RK (Nepal); Jan). viii) The High Court would therefore only exercise its supervisory judicial review powers in special or exceptional cases (Lim; RK (Nepal); Jan). . . .) The mere fact that Parliament has chosen to introduce an appellate procedure which can operate harshly, for example in relation to out-of-country appeals, is not in itself a special or exceptional reason for the High Court to assume jurisdiction. Were it otherwise the system of out-of-country appeals would be rendered toothless given that in many cases the out-of-country procedure operates to the disadvantage of the appellant. If this were a factor militating in favour of judicial review that would serve to trigger a judicial review in the vast majority (if not all) section 10 cases (Lim; RK (Nepal); Jan). The same applies where the High Court takes the view that it is more effective and convenient for it to hear the case; this is however not a good reason to assume jurisdiction (Willford)."—*R. (on the application of Khan) v Secretary of State for the Home Department* [2014] EWHC 2494 (Admin).
[81a] [2013] EWHC 2512 (Admin).

22. There is a string of ouster clause cases. These are concerned with the issue of finality, the exclusion of any further court review of a decision. There are several authorities where the ouster precedents have been distinguished. *Farley v Secretary of State for Work and Pensions (No 2)* [2006] UKHL 31; [2006] 1 W.L.R. 1817 is one. There the relevant statutory provision was section 33(4) of the Child Support Act 1991. Under it the Secretary of State could apply to a magistrates' court for a liability order in circumstances where the non-resident parent had failed to make maintenance payments. On such an application the section provided that the magistrates' court had to proceed on the basis that the maintenance assessment in question was lawfully and properly made. The House of Lords held that section 33(4) was not an ouster clause, but was part of a statutory scheme which allocated jurisdiction to determine the validity of an assessment elsewhere than at the stage when a liability order was before the magistrates' court. Thus section 33(4) did not have to be interpreted with the strictness appropriate to a provision which, as in Anisminic, purported to exclude the jurisdiction of the court to determine whether a ministerial order was a nullity. Lord Nicholls (with whom the other law lords agreed) said: 'This strict approach [Anisminic], however, is not appropriate if an effective means of challenging the validity of a maintenance assessment is provided elsewhere. Then section 33(4) is not an ouster provision': [18]. He went on to find that when in force, certain statutory provisions offered an effective means by which an absent parent could challenge the Secretary of State's jurisdiction to make a maintenance assessment: [20], [25]."

Non-interference with jurisdiction

19.1.22.1.3 *[New paragraph]*

From the fact that the courts begin with a presumption that legislation does not intend to remove judicial jurisdiction, it follows that they will operate an even stronger presumption that a power to make secondary legislation conferred by primary legislation does not intend to confer the power to remove judicial jurisdiction.[81b]

[81b] See, for example: "Does s.124 of the Finance Act 2008 contain words of sufficient clarity to forewarn that a right of appeal from First-tier Tribunal to Upper Tribunal was to be withdrawn? There can be no dispute as to the manner in which the power may be exercised. Provisions may amend repeal or revoke any provision of any Act (S.124 (6)). But the point is not the manner in which the power may be exercised but the matter for which provision may be made. ... A benevolent construction might, at a stretch, include, within the meaning of a 'provision as to the circumstances in which an appeal may be made', the abolition of a right of appeal where the subject-matter is the circumstances in which an appeal may be entertained. It might even, at a stretch, include, within the meaning of a provision 'in connection with an appeal against an HMRC decision', abolition of the right of appeal against a decision of the First-tier tribunal, where that subject-matter is in issue. But the need for clear words precludes any such benevolence. ... I conclude that s.124 did not give a power to revoke the right of appeal, conferred by s.11 of TCEA 2009, from the First-tier Tribunal to

the Upper Tribunal in relation to hardship decisions. Paragraph 221(5) is ultra vires. . . . In JCWI asylum seekers' rights of application and appeal conferred by primary legislation were rendered nugatory by regulations restricting their right to urgent benefits. But provided the power conferred by one statute to amend the provisions of another by delegated legislation is clear and express so that it is plain that Parliament understood the nature and scope of the power it was conferring on the executive, there is no reason in principle why the statute should not do so. . . . I would rule that the insertion of s.84(3C) by paragraph 221(5) was ultra vires."—*R. (on the application of ToTel Ltd) v The First-tier Tribunal (Tax Chamber)* [2012] EWCA Civ 1401.

OTHER CANONS AND PRINCIPLES OF CONSTRUCTION

Introduction

[Insert at end of table]

Principle of legality   Para.20.1.8.1

Purpose of canons

[New paragraph]

 Although they continue to serve a useful purpose in deconstructing legislation in a controlled and uniform way, there is a general feeling that many of the older separate canons of interpretation are gradually being merged into a general purposive approach.[4a]

 [4a] See, for example, "Lewison LJ found support for that submission in the principle that in statutory construction the specific overrides the general—generalia specialibus non derogant (see eg *Pretty v Solly* (1859) 26 Beav 606 53 ER 1032). In his view, the council's proposed action and the reason for taking it 'fall squarely within section 66(2)', and accordingly section 80 did not apply to the facts of the case (para 21). He considered an alternative argument based on section 3 of the Human Rights Act 1998, but did not think that argument took Mr Cusack's case any further (para 27). 10. In this court Mr Sauvain for the council challenges that conclusion. There is no justification, he says, for application of the general/specific principle where there is no conflict between the two provisions. Although they may overlap, they are provided for different purposes and apply in different situations. Where the council has two alternative statutory methods of achieving the same objective, it is entitled to adopt the one which imposes the least burden on the public purse (*Westminster Bank Ltd v Minister of Housing and Local Government* [1971] A.C. 508, 530). Whether compensation is payable depends on the particular statutory provision. 11. Mr Green, as I understood his arguments in this court, relied less on the general/specific principle as such, than on a purposive interpretation of the statutory provisions in their context. Although he put his arguments in a number of ways, the common theme was that the broad, unfettered power asserted by the council, without the protection of compensation, was irreconcilable with the general scheme of the Act and the pattern of other comparable provisions. In particular the council's construction of section 80 would enable it to override the safeguards provided in other sections. In particular, it would deprive section 66(2) of most of its apparent content, and, if applied to footpaths and bridleways, would enable it to bypass the prohibition on the use of section 66 to obstruct a private access (section 66(3)(5))."—*Cusack v London Borough of Harrow* [2013] UKSC 40.

Principle of legality

20.1.8.2 *[New paragraph]*

As discussed above,[27a] principles based on the protection of fundamental rights and the requirement to govern and legislate fairly are entrenched in the legal system of the United Kingdom, and have been entrenched long before the enactment of the Human Rights Act 1998.

This gives rise to a rebuttable presumption operated by the courts that legislation is not intended to interfere with fundamental rights. That notion is sometimes expressed as the principle of legality:

> "23. The principle of legality is that fundamental rights cannot be over-ridden by general or ambiguous statutory words: see per Lord Hoffmann in *R v Secretary of State for the Home Department, ex parte Simms* [2000] 2 A.C. 115, 131. In *Ex parte Simms*, the question was whether section 47(1) of the Prison Act 1952 enabled the Secretary of State to make rules restricting the fundamental right of prisoners to communicate with journalists. The subsection enabled the making of rules for, amongst other things, 'the regulation and management of prisons ... and for the classification, treatment, employment, discipline and control of persons required to be detained therein'. It was held by the House of Lords that this general power to make rules for the regulation and management of prisons was insufficiently clear to authorise the infringement of the basic rights of prisoners."[27b]

The principle of legality will not be allowed to interfere with the achievement of clear legislative objectives:

> "64. Fourth, as we have already said, any defence provided to those who assist someone to die would have to apply not merely to euthanasia but also to assisted suicide. That immediately raises the question: how can the courts develop a defence to assisted suicide when Parliament has stated in unequivocal terms that it is a serious criminal offence carrying a maximum sentence of 14 years' imprisonment. Mr Bowen sought to rely on the principle of legality, as it is sometimes called, which began to gain traction in the period leading up to the introduction of the Human Rights Act. The principle was expressed in the following terms by Lord Hoffmann in *R v Secretary of State for the Home Department ex p. Simms* [2002] 2 A.C. 115,131:

[27a] See Ch.11, Section 3.
[27b] *AJA v Commissioner of Police for the Metropolis* [2013] EWCA Civ 1342.

'Parliamentary sovereignty means that Parliament can, if it chooses, legislate contrary to fundamental principles of human rights. The Human Rights Act 1998 will not detract from this power. The constraints upon its exercise by Parliament are ultimately political, not legal. But the principle of legality means that Parliament must squarely confront what it is doing and accept the political cost. Fundamental rights cannot be overridden by general or ambiguous words. This is because there is too great a risk that the full implications of their unqualified meaning may have passed unnoticed in the democratic process. In the absence of express language or necessary implication to the contrary, the courts therefore presume that even the most general words were intended to be subject to the basic rights of the individual. In this way the courts of the United Kingdom, though acknowledging the sovereignty of Parliament, apply principles of constitutionality little different from those which exist in countries where the power of the legislature is expressly limited by a constitutional document.'

65. This principle of statutory interpretation has been adopted in a number of cases to read down general words where precise and well established fundamental rights have been in issue. These have included the right of unimpeded access to the courts: *R v Lord Chancellor ex-parte Witham* [1998] QB 575; the right not to be punished by retrospective legislation: *Waddington v Miah* [1974] 1 W.L.R. 683; the right not to have penalties increased: *R v Secretary of State for the Home Department ex-parte Pierson* [1998] A.C. 539 (HL); and the right to communicate confidentially with a legal advisor under the principle of legal professional privilege: *R (On the Application of Daly) v SSHD* [2001] 2 A.C. 532. It is to be noted that they are all detailed and specific rights.

66. In our judgment, this principle of statutory construction could not conceivably have any application here, for two quite distinct reasons. First, as we have noted, there is no right—let alone a fundamental right—to commit suicide, and the right to assist someone to do so cannot place the party providing assistance in a stronger position than the party committing suicide. Second, section 2(2) of the Suicide Act is not ambiguous, nor is it cast in general terms. There is no scope for giving it a limited interpretation. There is no conceivable risk that Parliament may not have understood the full implications of a blanket ban, or that the problems of those unable to commit suicide have passed unnoticed in the democratic process. On the contrary, Parliament fully understood what a blanket ban meant and why they were imposing it. They have on numerous occasions considered specific proposals for change but have so far chosen not to accede to them. The principle of legality can gain no hold here. This difficulty alone is in our view decisive of this submission. If a defence of necessity cannot be fashioned for assisted suicide, it certainly cannot for euthanasia."— *R. (on*

111

the application of Nicklinson) v Ministry of Justice [2013] EWCA Civ 961.

Casus omissus

20.1.16 *[Insert at end of note 49]*

; see also, "141. These speeches demonstrate that not all holes (if identified) can be filled by the courts. The present case may or may not demonstrate a hole, but if it does then it is one which, similarly, cannot be filled by what is otherwise a forced and illegitimate process of construction of words in the Act which are lighted on for that purpose."—*Westbrook Dolphin Square Ltd v Friends Life Ltd* [2014] EWHC 2433 (Ch).

Presumption of meaning

20.1.23 *[Insert at end of note 71]*

; see also, "But even if 'generally' is surplusage, that is insufficient of itself to point to one interpretation rather than another. First, the policy should not be construed with the rigour that is applied to the interpretation of statutes which have been drafted by Parliamentary draftsmen and contracts which have been drafted by lawyers. Secondly, even in the context of statutes and contracts, arguments based on surplusage are rarely of much force: see *Arbuthnot v Fagan* [1995] CLC 1396, 1404 (per Hoffmann LJ) and *Beaufort Developments (NI) Ltd v Gilbert Ash NI Ltd* [1999] 1 A.C. 266, 274B (per Lord Hoffmann)."—*Ashburton Trading Ltd v Secretary of State for Communities and Local Government* [2014] EWCA Civ 378.

Presumption of correct law

20.1.37 *[Insert at end of note 111]*

; see also—"65. I accept that Parliament must be taken to have been aware by 2011 of the decision in Smith. But a Court of Appeal decision solely based on the effect of the existence of public rights of way over the land, and not endorsing or rejecting what HHJ Pelling said about the effect of the trespass by highway obstruction being an offence, should not be taken as showing that Parliament must have realised that the past and future effect of criminalising trespass was that title by adverse possession could not then be obtained."—*Best v The Chief Land Registrar* [2014] EWHC 1370 (Admin).

20.1.37A *[New paragraph]*

The presumption does not prevent the courts from inquiring into, and testing, any fundamental assumptions that the legislature appears to have made in framing legislation, and drawing appropriate conclusions in relation to its interpretation.[112a]

This topic is linked to the fact that the legislature is not taken to have power to make implied declarations as to the state of the law.[112b]

With the increasing tendency of the courts to have regard to parliamentary history and to inquire into the assumptions and attitudes of the legislature in forming a view of the legislative intent,[112c] it is probably fair to say that to the extent that the presumption of correct law implies some kind of deference to the legislature, that deference has significantly diminished in recent years. While the Bill of Rights, art.9 continues to prevent the courts from "judging" the accuracy or efficacy of the legislature's deliberations in framing legislation, the growth of exceptions to the rule caused by European Union and human rights considerations have made the courts more prepared to analyse the legislature's deliberations in a way that would itself have once been thought unconstitutional. It is a relatively short step from exposing the shortcomings in the legislature's analysis

---

[112a] See, for example, "The question here is whether section 9(2) is applicable to the right of pre-emption and, if it is, whether the relevant 21 year perpetuity period has expired. If it is applicable and the period has expired the right of pre-emption is void for remoteness and, what is more, is to be treated as void also as between the BBC and Council (as the persons by whom and in whose favour it was made). This is by force of section 10 of the 1964 Act. . . . The critical question as regards the application of section 9(2) is to understand what is meant by the phrase 'option to acquire for valuable consideration any interest in land'. Does it mean an option as understood in *Gomm* and like decisions? Or does it have an extended meaning and, if it does, what is the nature of that extended meaning? It is at this point that the distinction between an option to acquire land and a right of pre-emption in respect of land comes into prominence. . . . In the light of the decision in *Pritchard v Briggs* I am of the view, indeed in the light of the reasoning that underlies that decision I doubt that it is open to me to come to a different view, that Parliament proceeded on a wrong assumption (namely that a right of pre-emption did indeed give rise to an immediate interest in land) and that it would not therefore be right to regard the legislation as amending the law by treating rights of pre-emption exceptionally as if they give rise to an immediate interest in land. Looking at the issue more generally, I can see no reason why, where the right in question sounds at the time of its creation only in contract and may never mature into a right which confers on the grantee an interest in land, Parliament should have wanted to single it out and treat it as if, from the moment of its creation, the right had this added proprietary effect. . . . Once it is accepted, as this alternative approach must do, that a right of pre-emption, so long as it has not matured into an option, is not within section 9(2) but only comes within the purview of the subsection (so that consideration of the perpetuity periods becomes relevant) once it matures into an option when the offer to sell is made, it is difficult to see why the relevant date for the starting of the perpetuity period must nevertheless be taken to be some earlier date. Clarity and the need for ease of application do not seem, with respect, to be a sufficient basis for doing so. On the contrary, the statutory provisions seem to me to point to the date when the option comes into existence (and the interest in the land arises) as being the relevant start date. What the subsection refers to is the disposition which confers the option to acquire the interest in the land. It would seem reasonably clear therefore that the date for measuring the 21-year perpetuity period is the date when the option arises rather than the date when the right of pre-emption is conferred. The fact that this may not be ascertainable by recourse to the date of a written instrument is by no means an argument against this view. It is to be noted that the definition of 'disposition' in section 15(6) of the 1964 Act provides for the case where the disposition is made 'otherwise than by an instrument.' In such a case the Act is to apply 'as if the disposition had been contained in an instrument taking effect when the disposition is made.' "—*Cosmichome Ltd v Southampton City Council* [2013] EWHC 1378 (Ch).

[112b] See paras 1.8.4–1.8.4.1.

[112c] See Ch.27.

of the pre-existing law to refusing to base the interpretation of the law on the legislature's misconceptions.

Cross-contextual construction

20.1.39.2 *[New paragraph]*

The courts will apply a cross-contextual construction only with caution. In particular, they will be careful to look for any reason why it is inappropriate having regard to the context of either of the provisions involved. Most obviously, the fact that a definition has been expressly defined in the context of one Act will make it difficult or impossible to persuade the courts to have regard to an earlier judicial construction in another context.[123a]

When amending legislation in a particular context the Government can of course express a view as to the extent to which it is or is not intended to have cross-contextual influence.[123b] However, it will be for the courts to determine whether that intention has been achieved. In keeping with the general rule that it is for the legislature to legislate and for the courts to apply and interpret, although the courts may have regard to the statement of the Government's intention, whether under the rule in *Pepper v Hart* or otherwise, they are unlikely to defer to it to any great extent; particularly since what is at stake is actually the interpretation of the other contexts and the legislative intent as to their interpretation and not the interpretation of the amending provision inserted by the Government in the new context.

Now that the United Kingdom is composed of three devolved legislatures in addition to the Westminster Parliament, there is additional scope for strong cross-contextual constructions where the same area is legislated for by different UK

[123a] See, for example: "Despite my request, the solicitor-advocate for the pursuers was unable to provide any precedent for approaching statutory interpretation in the way which he proposed. He made some reference to the reasoning of Lord Reid in *Watson v Fram Reinforced Concrete Co (Scotland)* 1960 S.C. (H.L.) at p107–108. That is of no assistance to the pursuers. The present case does not deal with a situation where words in an old statute have been interpreted by the courts in a particular way and then the words have been used again in a later Act. It was in that situation that Lord Reid stated the words should be interpreted in the same way. Lord Reid was not referring to a situation, as in the present case, where Parliament has provided a particular definition for a term to apply in a particular Act."—*Anton v South Ayrshire Council* [2012] CSOH 80.

[123b] "My noble friend Lady Hamwee in tabling her amendments, and the noble Baroness, Lady Walmsley, in speaking to them, sought an assurance that introducing into Section 1 an explicit reference to psychological harm will not mean that references to suffering or injury in other legislation will be read as not extending to psychological harm—in other words, that there is no extension of the concept that we are seeking to put right here to other legislation. I can assure my noble friend that Clause 62 is intended only to clarify the meaning of suffering or injury in the context of Section 1 of the 1933 Act. It reflects the Government's view that the term already includes, by implication, suffering or injury of a psychological nature. It is not intended to change any other statute by implication."—Serious Crime Bill 2014–15—*http://www.publications.parliament.uk/pa/ld201415/ldhansrd/text/140715-0001.htm#14071553000431*.

legislatures (subject to the need to guard against clearly intentional differences of policy).[123c]

[New paragraph]   **20.1.39.3**

Even where a definition is expressly constrained by words that indicate that it is intended to apply only "in this Act" or by some similar limitation, that does not mean that the courts will necessarily feel unable to effect a cross-contextual construction. In particular, there is a presumption of consistency by virtue of which the courts will assume, unless the contrary is shown, that when the legislature operates in an area where there is already legislation, the new legislation will be enacted in the knowledge of the existing legislation and will reflect its key principles and terminology unless there is a good reason for departing from them.[123d]

[123c] See, for example: "[23] I am also wary, in the absence of compelling evidence, of drawing a significant distinction between the wording of statutes passed by two different legislative bodies in different jurisdictions when each piece of legislation is intended to reverse the effect of the House of Lords decision. Reading Section 1(1) and (2) of the 2011 Act together, I conclude that pleural plaques is now a statutory personal injury for which damages can and should be awarded if the plaintiff proves fault against the defendant."—*McCauley v Harland and Wolff Plc* [2014] NIQB 91.

[123d] See, for example, "14. Mr Southey relies, as I have foreshadowed, on the fact that section 76(1) opens with the words 'In this Act', so that, as he would put it, the definition of 'custodial sentence' as 'sentence of imprisonment' is limited to the 2000 Act. But the 2003 Act was enacted in the knowledge of the careful regime provided for in section 76 and 85 of the 2000 Act. If it was intended that the reference to a prison sentence in the 2003 Act meant something different from the meaning given in section 76, the plain expectation is that the legislature would have said so. 15.The starting point for any sensible consideration of a question of this kind is the proposition that Parliament may be taken to have acted consistently. The submission also advanced this morning that the seriousness of the offence is reflected or given by the custodial term strictly and not the extension period (itself with great respect a doubtful proposition, pace a comment of Leveson LJ to which we were referred in *R v H* [2007] EWCA Crim 2622 at paragraph 18) does nothing, in my view, to touch the relationship between the statutory provisions with which we are here concerned. The notification requirements are not merely concerned with the gravity of the offence in terms of the offender's culpability; they are concerned with risk, protection and prevention. In short there is nothing in any consideration of the statutes to displace the conclusion of the Divisional Court."—*Minter v Hampshire Constabulary* [2013] EWCA Civ 697.

CHAPTER 21

EXPRESSIONS WHICH CHANGE MEANING OVER TIME

[Insert at end of note 3]   **21.1.1**

; see also—"I take the view that one can apply the 'always speaking' approach to statutory construction to the provisions of the Schedule to the CFO, although we are not called upon on this appeal to express any view as to whether, so interpreted, they were satisfied by airlines other than Ryanair in the period under review. But I am also satisfied that, whether or not they can be so interpreted, the correct approach to construction is not to delete Notes (5)(b) and (6) from the Schedule. Lord Pannick's point that some support for Ryanair's construction can be derived from the present impossibility of literal compliance with the conjunction tickets provisions is, I think, misplaced. The CFO cannot be construed by reference to subsequent events which were not necessarily foreseeable in 1994 and, when looked at in the context of the ticketing practices at that time, its provisions were entirely workable."—*Ryanair Ltd v HM Revenue and Customs* [2014] EWCA Civ 410; as to the fundamental justification for the modern presumption, see, for example: "45. It is not difficult to see why an updating construction of legislation is generally to be preferred. Legislation is not and could not be constantly re-enacted and is generally expected to remain in place indefinitely, until it is repealed, for what may be a long period of time. An inevitable corollary of this is that the circumstances in which a law has to be applied may differ significantly from those which existed when the law was made—as a result of changes in technology or in society or in other conditions. This is something which the legislature may be taken to have had in contemplation when the law was made. If the question is asked "is it reasonable to suppose that the legislature intended a court applying the law in the future to ignore such changes and to act as if the world had remained static since the legislation was enacted?", the answer must generally be 'no'. A 'historical' approach of that kind would usually be perverse and would defeat the purpose of the legislation."—*R. (on the application of N) v Walsall MBC*; *sub nom. R. (on the application of ZYN) v Walsall MBC* [2014] EWHC 1918 (Admin).

[New paragraph]   **21.1.7**

The principle of statutes being construed in an "always speaking" manner is capable of spanning centuries, with the legislative intent being construed in a way that works for one century in accordance with the original policy intentions.[31]

The essential process of determining whether or not to apply an "always speaking" construction involves accurate identification of the original legislative intent of the statute, following which it should be relatively easy to determine what terminological and other developments fall naturally to be embraced by the original legislative purpose.[32]

---

[31] See, for example: "22. The principle that a statute is 'always speaking' is not disputed. In the context of statutory provisions granting tax exemptions it was confirmed in *Associated Newspapers Ltd. v Corporation of the City of London* [1916] 2 A.C. 429. The case concerned land that had been enclosed and reclaimed from the River Thames following the enactment of a statute in 1767 whose purpose was to make a number of improvements to the City of London: 7 Geo. 3. c. 37. It included the completion of Blackfriars Bridge and the embanking of part of the north side of the river. To encourage private landowners to carry the burden of the cost of reclaiming land nearby, section 51 of that Act provided that the ground and soil enclosed and embanked in front of each existing wharf or ground would vest in the owner and be 'free from all taxes and assessments whatsoever'. The House of Lords rejected an argument that the exemption (which was assumed to cover local taxes and assessments alone) applied only to such taxes as existed at the time of Royal Assent. It applied to all local taxes and assessments whether present or future."—*R. (on the application of the Company of Proprietors of Whitchurch Bridge) v HM Treasury* [2012] EWHC 3579 (Admin).

[32] See, for example, "21. The Board drew attention to the guiding principle when a new activity is said to fall within old statutory language. It is to be found in Lord Bingham's endorsement (in *R (Quintavalle) v Health Secretary* [2003] 2 A.C. 687 [10]) of the dissenting opinion of Lord Wilberforce in *Royal College of Nursing of the United Kingdom v Department of Health and Social Security* [1981] A.C. 800, 822 (cited at length in the judgment below at [24]) Is the new activity within the genus of the statutory definitions? Is the inclusion of the new activity consistent with the purpose of the statute? 22. It is not difficult to identify a statutory purpose; Parliament intended to permit the Board to impose a levy on bookmakers and not on their customers. Under a statutory scheme which distinguishes between bookmakers, on whom the levy may be imposed, and their customers, who place bets, on whom no levy may be imposed, it is not possible to do away with that distinction and say that the customers are also bookmakers. Parliament maintained that distinction even after it recognised and made provisions in relation to betting exchanges (see s.5AB of the Betting and Gaming Duties Act 1981, q.v. infra [40])."—*R. (on the application of William Hill Organisation Ltd) v Horserace Betting Levy Board* [2013] EWCA Civ 487.

CHAPTER 22

THE INTERPRETATION ACT 1978

Section 7: service by post

[New paragraph]   **22.1.12.2**

For analysis of the existing authorities on, and application of, s.7, see *Freetown v Assethold Ltd.*[34a]

Section 9: references to time of day

[Insert new paragraph at end of note 36]   **22.1.14**

See also: "[21] The court had some unease about whether the respondent had complied with the strict provisions of Article 40 of the 1996 Order i.e. the requirement to give a written itemised pay statement. However, in his submission Mr Warnock drew our attention to section 46(1) of the Interpretation (NI) Act 1954 which provides: "'Writing', 'written' or any term of like import shall include words typewritten, printed, painted, engraved, lithographed, photographed or represented or reproduced by any mode of representing or reproducing words in a visible form." [22] We accept that in the context of current standards of information technology the requirement to provide a written itemised pay statement is complied with if words are reproduced in a visible form on a computer screen. To that however we would add this caveat—if an employer is aware that an employee is having difficulty of any sort in actually accessing a payslip in this way, the employer is obliged to find an alternative method of providing information in accordance with the statutory requirement. Notwithstanding this caveat we agree that the Tribunal was correct in law to dismiss this aspect of the appellant's claim."—*Anakaa v Firstsource Solutions Ltd* [2014] NICA 57.

[34a] [2012] EWCA Civ 1657; an extensive extract of the judgment in that case appears in Annex A to this Supplement.

CHAPTER 24

OTHER SPECIFIC INTERPRETATION PROVISIONS

Circular definitions

[New paragraph]   **24.1.5.2**

A definition that depends for its meaning on a provision of itself becomes circular and devoid of effect.[11a] One might think that this was so obvious that it could readily be avoided by the drafter. The reality is that this is a heffalump trap, the floor of which is more thickly populated with unwary woozles than one might expect. The trap is particularly difficult to spot where the definition is distributed between more than one provision and the separated parts are inter-dependent.

[11a] See, for example: "'Distribute' in Section 4(4) fares little better. It is a circular definition: 'Distribute . . . means distribute by means of a distribution system' So distribute means distribute means distribute. A hint as to the meaning is given by the explanation that distribution is through a 'system' which is something used for 'conveying electricity', which can be taken to suggest that distribute connotes a purely physical transport or conveyance function. In the Directive 'Distribution' is pithily defined as 'transport' and the unequivocal qualification is added 'but does not include supply' (see paragraph [80] above). However, the domestic equivalent does not make this clear."—*R. (on the application of UK Power Networks Services (Contracting) Ltd) v Gas and Electricity Markets Authority* [2014] EWHC 3678 (Admin).

CHAPTER 25

SECTION 3 OF THE HUMAN RIGHTS ACT 1998

Application of the rule

[Insert at end of note 30]   **25.1.7**

; see also, for example: "45. I fear that this concentration on the thrust of the legislation misses the point. As Lord Rodger said in *Ghaidan* at [110], 'however powerful the obligation in section 3(1) may be, it does not allow the courts to change the substance of a provision completely, to change a provision from one where Parliament says that x is to happen into one saying that x is not to happen'. In my opinion, that is the trap into which the CAC fell. Once para. 3(6) had said in express terms that the definition of the phrase 'collective bargaining' in para. 3(3) was not to apply to the phrase 'collective bargaining' in para. 35, i.e. once para. 3(6) had expressly prohibited the phrase 'collective bargaining' in para. 35 from meaning 'negotiations relating to pay, hours and holidays', it was not open to the CAC to add words to para. 35 to say that that was what the phrase 'collective bargaining' in para. 35 does mean. The CAC should have given effect to para. 35 in accordance with its terms, even if that meant that the PDAU's right to engage in collective bargaining by invoking the Schedule was being violated."—*R. (on the application of Boots Management Services Ltd) v Central Arbitration Committee* [2014] EWHC 65 (Admin).

CHAPTER 26

USE OF PARTS OF LEGISLATION OTHER THAN TEXT FOR CONSTRUCTION

Headings

[New paragraph]   **26.1.11.2.1**

Although the courts will therefore be prepared to have fairly free regard to headings for the purposes of statutory construction—and it is probably true to say that they feel increasingly free to do so from year to year—they are still on their guard against allowing headings to deflect them from what would otherwise be the inescapable, even if undesirable, conclusion as to the meaning of a provision.[47a]

[47a] See, for example: "We accept that the subheading of this section, 'Defendant neither convicted nor acquitted', may be considered to be at variance with such an interpretation. However, we see no reason to believe that the time at which an accused is 'neither convicted nor acquitted' is necessarily referable to the date of the making of the confiscation order and may equally well refer to the date when an accused absconds. 22. Moreover, as Lord Reid observed in *DPP v Schildkamp* [1971] A.C. 1: i. 'The side note is a poor guide to the scope of a section, for it can do no more than indicate the main subject with which the section deals.' "—*R. v Okedare (Charles)* [2014] EWCA Crim 1173.

CHAPTER 27

USE OF EXTRANEOUS MATERIAL

Dictionaries

[*New paragraph*]   **27.1.2.2**

There is a danger in using a dictionary definition in that it can cause the reader to concentrate more on a notional "neutral" meaning of the defined term, and therefore less on the contextual meaning of the term in the light of the background and intention of the surrounding provision.[19a]

Explanatory notes to Acts

[*New paragraph*]   **27.1.7.2A**

For a case where the court refused to read a provision of a statutory instrument as having the meaning specified in the Explanatory Note, see *Santander UK Plc v Harrison.*[53a]

[*New paragraph*]   **27.1.7.2.1**

The courts have been at pains to discourage too slavish a reliance on assertions and assurances in Explanatory Notes: see, in particular:

"The statement of Lord Steyn does no more than create a category of case where statements made prior to legislation become admissible. Lord Steyn was at pains to point out that the mere fact that a clear assurance in an

---

[19a] See, for example: "23. I doubt whether, with respect to the District Judge, help is to be gained from the dictionary. Indeed, there is a danger in its use since by lighting on a dictionary definition, the force of the word used in the section is diminished. Looking up the dictionary to find synonyms does not assist in understanding the meaning of the word 'intimidating' in the context of s.68(1). I share Lord Upjohn's view that it is highly dangerous, if not impossible, to attempt to place an accurate definition upon a word in common use; 'you can look up examples of its many uses if you want to in your Oxford Dictionary, but that does not help on definition' (*Customs & Excise Commissioners v Top Ten Promotions Limited* [1969] 1 W.L.R. 1163 at 1171.)"—*Bauer v The Director of Public Prosecutions* [2013] EWHC 634 (Admin).
[53a] [2013] EWHC 199 (QB).

Explanatory Note could be read as an 'assurance' could not, without more, be taken to reflect the will of Parliament. And this must be right. Although in many, if not most, instances the view of the Executive can be expected to be reflected in the subsequent enactment of Parliament this is not an a fortiori equation. Parliament is sovereign and its views are constitutionally discrete from those of the Executive. The gap can in some cases, however, be bridged as explained by Lord Carswell in *R v Z* (see at paragraph [50] above) to the effect that where there is a very clear pre-legislative statement which turns out to be inconsistent with the subsequent enactment the latter may be construed to mean the same as the former where this can properly be said to reflect the will of Parliament. In such a case the view of the Executive is not taking precedence over that of Parliament; it is simply that the earlier statement is said on analysis to be an accurate reflection of Parliament's will. At base this approach by the Court seeks to override infelicitous statutory language which the Court concludes is not a proper reflection of Parliament's actual will and it is aided in this endeavour by reference to admissible pre-legislative material. I would make five observations about this approach. First, the pre-existing statements relied upon must be exceptionally clear and precise and amount to something which can be understood as an "assurance". Second, there can be no quick and easy assumption that Parliament necessarily intended to respect this assurance if in fact it uses language which is inconsistent with the assurance (as Mr Michael Fordham QC quite fairly accepted). Third, the Court must therefore be satisfied that the prior assurance does in fact and law accurately reflect Parliament's will. Fourth, in Westminster City Council Lord Steyn was concerned only with Explanatory Notes as a guide to interpretation, nothing else. However, it seems to me that the underlying principle can be applied both to (a) any form of pre-legislative material which in law is admissible; and (b) to the process of identifying the purpose of Parliament in an enactment. Fifth, there is a tension in this area with normal *Pepper v Hart* principles which militate against the admissibility of pre-legislative material as guides to interpretation and in the relevant cases the courts have sought to square the *Pepper v Hart* circle with some finely tuned analysis. All of this suggests that the circumstances in which a pre-legislative assurance will be treated as reflecting Parliament's when this is not apparent from the enactment (and even more so when it is inconsistent) may be exceptional.

I now apply those principles to the facts of the present case. First, I do not construe the Explanatory Notes as creating any form of assurance. I have set out my analysis of this at paragraph [60] above. Second, equally I do not construe the statement of the Minister in Parliament as creating any form of representation which could be elevated into an assurance of the sort that Lord Steyn was referring to (see paragraphs [57]–[59] above). And further as to the statements made in White Papers and consultation documents these would, on Lord Steyn's analysis, carry materially less weight than Explanatory Notes or a direct statement by a sponsoring Minister. But in any event these admittedly clear statements of intent were not and could not be construed as "assurances". They reflected the policy of the moment which whilst firm was always capable of reversal and the constraints in the LCF represented inescapable context."[53b]

The courts have also been resistant to the suggestion that the Explanatory Notes can acquire sufficient authority to supply significant deficiencies in the text of the legislation:

"22. I am called upon to construe the statute and not the Explanatory Note. The Explanatory Note may itself be explained by the reference to prizes in the bingo duty provisions in s.20 of the Betting and Gaming Duties Act 1981 as amended. But whether it can be explained or not, I cannot believe that the draughtsman sought to introduce so substantial an amendment in so opaque and coy a manner."[53c]

Consultation paper prior to legislation

[New paragraph]   27.1.11.A1

It may now be taken as settled law that consultation papers and similar materials are admissible in evidence of the legislative intent of legislation which arises out of them; but the courts will exercise caution in determining what weight to give to material of that kind once admitted.[66a]

[53b] *Solar Century Holdings Ltd v Secretary of State for Energy & Climate Change* [2014] EWHC 3677 (Admin).

[53c] *Aspinalls Club Ltd v Revenue and Customs Commissioners* [2013] EWCA Civ 1464.

[66a] See, for example: "21. Mr. Bhose also sought to rely on a consultation paper issued by the Office of the Deputy Prime Minister on the proposed regulations in August 2002, which was referred to by Lord Wilson JSC in his dissenting judgment in *Daejan* at paragraph 109, albeit for a different purpose. Mr. Bhose relied on *Craies on Legislation*, 10th ed., 2012 at paragraph 27.1.11, for the proposition that such papers can be relevant evidence for the construction of legislation although—as Lord Steyn said, pertinently to the present case, in his dissenting speech in *R. on the application of Eddison First Limited. Central Valuation Officer* [2003] 4 All E..R. 209: 'The question is how far, on a contextual reading of a statute, the language is capable of stretching'. 22. I am satisfied that both the Regulations and the consultation paper (which contain the same provision that became Regulation 3(l)(d) in the attached draft regulations, except that there was no exemption for agreements for less than 5 years) are admissible in evidence, on the ground that they were sufficiently contemporaneous with the Act. The legislation received the Royal Assent on 1st May 2002, the draft regulations were in existence by 17th July 2002 and were attached to the consultation paper in August 2002. It is also clear that the Act and the Regulations were intended to be part of one code. It does not, of course, follow that the understanding of the civil servant(s) who drafted the Regulations and wrote the consultation paper (who may or may not be the same person) represents the intention of the legislation which was drafted by a Parliamentary draftsman. One simply cannot know the extent of the consultation on the relevant point at issue, if any, between the persons concerned. It is always necessary to keep in mind the practical reality, that the person drafting subordinate legislation, or other admissible documents such as a consultation paper, may simply have misunderstood the meaning of the Act. Where, as here, there is really little doubt as to the meaning of the Act, and considerable stretching of the language required to produce an ambiguity, the Regulations and any

Draft Bills

27.1.11.2   [*New paragraph*]

Draft Bills may also on occasion be considered by the courts as evidence of the perceived need for changes in the law. That will not of course be taken as determinative that the perceived defect does in fact exist—that is a matter for the courts to determine for themselves. However, it may shed light on the general perception and application of a particular provision, including its limitations.[71a]

Opinion of Minister or Department after enactment of legislation for construction purposes

27.1.12.3   [*Insert at end of note 80*]

; see also—"30. The views of the DTI, as it then was, as to the meaning of the Regulations are not in my view relevant."—*Shearman (t/a Charles Shearman Agencies) v Hunter Boot Ltd* [2014] EWHC 47 (QB).

Opinions of Parliamentary Select Committees

27.1.13.3   [*New paragraph*]

For another example of the courts' willingness to have regard to Parliamentary Reports for the purposes of legislative construction see:

---

other admissible documents are likely to be of very little weight."—"9. The issue to be decided is whether the term 'the landlord' in the definition of 'qualifying long term agreement' in section 20ZA means anyone who is, or who at any later time becomes, a landlord. ... Again, it is difficult to imagine that, if it had been intended that potential future landlords would be obliged to seek dispensation from the LVT, this would not have been explicitly provided for, and one would have expected provision for regulations to be issued governing the procedure before the LVT on such a one-sided application. I do not think that what Lewison J. said in *Paddington Basin Developments* is of any assistance in this case; plainly he was not contemplating the present, very different, case now before the court, in which all consultation is impossible."—*BDW Trading Ltd v South Anglia Housing Ltd* [2013] EWHC B10 (Ch).

[71a] "No doubt mindful of their obligations under article 4, the UK authorities are striving in various ways to combat trafficking and to protect its victims. I refer, for example, to the Draft Modern Slavery Bill, Cm 8770, presented to Parliament in December 2013 and in particular to the amendments to it proposed by the government in its paper, Cm 8889, presented in June 2014 by way of response to the report of a parliamentary committee on the draft Bill. I note, for example, that one such amendment would provide a statutory defence to a victim of trafficking who, as a result, has been compelled to commit a crime. Although Miss Hounga is not in that category, the decision of the Court of Appeal to uphold Mrs Allen's defence of illegality to her complaint runs strikingly counter to the prominent strain of current public policy against trafficking and in favour of the protection of its victims. The public policy in support of the application of that defence, to the extent that it exists at all, should give way to the public policy to which its application is an affront; and Miss Hounga's appeal should be allowed."—*Hounga v Allen* [2014] UKSC 47.

"74. Mr Straw draws support for that approach from the report of the Joint Committee on Human Rights, Legislative Scrutiny, 15th Report, Session 2007–2008 which advances this interpretation of Article 2."[94a]

It is doubtful whether the courts would recognise that the rules relating to the use of Select Committee Reports have changed; but they would probably recognise, at least, that they have become more comfortable with the notion of comparing their reasoning with the opinions of Select Committees for reassurance, while not investing those Reports with any kind of interpretative authority.[94b] What is lacking, however, is any thematic treatment by the higher courts of what degree of attention they can give to Select Committee Reports without it amounting to infraction of Parliamentary Privilege under art.IX of the Bill of Rights; for the present, the courts simply appear to be gradually expanding their use of Parliamentary material without stopping to consider the correct limitations on its use or the potential constitutional implications of their failure to articulate or confirm clear limitations.

Legislative or parliamentary history

[New paragraph]   **27.1.14.5**

As a general rule, the courts appear to be allowing themselves increasing latitude to discuss details of legislative history of an Act, including arguments

---

[94a] *R. (on the application of Duggan) v HM Assistant Deputy Coroner for the Northern District of Greater London* [2014] EWHC 3343 (Admin); see also—"Whilst these proceedings were under way, the House of Commons Justice Committee conducted an inquiry into the appropriateness of the decision made on the 4th December 2013. The inquiry considered how the review pursuant to Section 48 had been carried out. At the conclusion of the hearing of these proceedings on the 30th July 2014 it was known that the Justice Committee's report was due to be published two days later. I indicated that I would consider the report when it had been published and that I would invite any submissions in relation to the content of the report if I considered this to be necessary or appropriate. Having considered the report after its publication, I concluded that no further submissions were required. I e-mailed the parties in these terms: 'As was anticipated on the 1st August 2014 the House of Commons Justice Committee issued its Third Report of the Session 2014–15 entitled Mesothelioma Claims. I have read the report. Many of the issues discussed in the report were raised in the evidence placed before me in the course of the judicial review proceedings and in the submissions made during the hearing on the 29th and 30th July 2014. I do not consider that it is necessary for any party to make further written submissions about the content of the report. As the Committee notes on page 14 of the report it is not its function to adjudicate on the Secretary of State's compliance with the relevant statutory requirement; rather its judgment is a political one. That political judgment may or may not lead to the same result as my judgment on the alleged breach by the Secretary of State of his statutory and public law duty. The report cannot inform my conclusion.' I do not need to expand on that e-mail. My reading of the report of the Justice Committee has not influenced my decision."—*R. (on the application of Whitston) v Secretary of State for Justice* [2014] EWHC 3044 (Admin); see also—"In that context Mr Eadie relied upon the observation of the Parliamentary Joint Committee on Human Rights that the objective of reducing long-term benefit dependency and encouraging people into work is 'potentially human rights-enhancing'."—*R. (on the application of JS) v Secretary of State for Work and Pensions* [2013] EWHC 3350 (QB).

[94b] See, for example, the careful treatment of the Select Committee on Statutory Instrument's discussion of an instrument in *Ryanair Ltd v HM Revenue and Customs* [2014] EWCA Civ 410.

over amendments made, withdrawn and defeated. In so far as *Pepper v Hart* was feared liked to "open the floodgates", the flood that it seems to have permitted is perhaps less in relation to the use of *Hansard* itself, and more in relation to general freedom to pray details of the Parliamentary proceedings on an enactment in aid of its interpretation.

The privilege of Parliament as encapsulated in art.9 of the Bill of Rights[109a] has traditionally been understood to require the courts to be extremely reluctant to consider aspects of an enactment's parliamentary passage, on the grounds that if it is open to one party to advance one implication of the parliamentary proceedings meaning it must be open to other parties to advance other implications, in which case it can become difficult or impossible for the courts to avoid "questioning" aspects of the parliamentary process. Despite this, the fashion of adverting to what did or did not happen in relation to particular amendments seems to become increasingly prevalent; but there are occasions on which judges express unease about the practical and constitutional implications.[109b]

[109a] Bill of Rights 1688 art.9: "That the Freedome of Speech and Debates or Proceedings in Parlyament ought not to be impeached or questioned in any Court or Place out of Parlyament."

[109b] See, for example: "The petitioner further placed some reliance on the debate in the House of Lords on the Bill that subsequently became the Legal Aid (Scotland) Act 1986. In *Hansard* for 6 March 1986, columns 352–354, it is recorded that discussion took place on an amendment to leave out the word "Scots" from the clause corresponding to the present section 6(1). The point made by Lord Morton of Shuna, who moved the amendment, was that advice should be available on the application of law in a situation where, for example, someone moved from Scotland to England in circumstances where matrimonial advice or contractual advice was required in respect of English law. The amendment was ultimately rejected. In the debate the Lord Advocate, Lord Cameron of Lochbroom, stated that the existing system worked satisfactorily and that it was difficult to see how a Scottish solicitor could give satisfactory advice on foreign law. Counsel for the petitioner suggested that this meant that the reason for confining the legal aid legislation to advice on Scots law was that a Scottish solicitor was not qualified to give advice on foreign law. That did not, however, apply to advice about the European Convention on Human Rights, because a Scottish solicitor was qualified to give such advice. While the latter point is no doubt correct so far as it goes, I am of opinion that the debate reveals that the reason for rejecting the amendment was more fundamental, namely that the existing system worked in a satisfactory manner. In any event, the fact that a Scottish solicitor is qualified to give advice on the Convention and to appear in the European Court of Human Rights does not in my view alter the fundamental meaning of the expression 'Scots law'. I am accordingly of opinion that there is no merit in this line of argument. This leads to the question how the courts should respond when interpreting legislation drafted in terms which, on a natural reading, may appear to catch conduct far wider than the mischief which Parliament had been invited to address. The decision in *Pepper v Hart* [1993] A.C. 593 was controversial and the courts have been generally cautious about looking at things said in Parliament as an aid to construction."—*Smith v R.* [2012] EWCA Crim 2566.

CHAPTER 28

THE RULE IN PEPPER v HART

The nature of Ministerial statements

[New paragraph]   **28.1.2.2**

As a rule there is no difficulty in determining when a Member of either House is speaking in a Ministerial capacity or as a private constituency MP or representative peer. However, instances of unclarity can arise. In particular, with a coalition government the courts may have the difficult job of determining whether a Minister speaks in their capacity as a Minister or in a party capacity.[10a]

The use made of the rule

[New paragraph]   **28.1.6.3**

Although the occasions on which *Pepper v Hart* has been decisive are few, for the reasons already discussed, it certainly cannot be dismissed by litigators as irrelevant in practice. There are certainly instances of decisions where judges have acknowledged expressly that their decision was at least potentially affected by a Ministerial statement.[39a]

[10a] See, for example, the debate on a clause of the Criminal Justice and Courts Bill on July 21, 2014 in the House of Lords—*http://www.publications.parliament.uk/pa/ld201415/ldhansrd/text/140721-0001.htm#1407215000847*.

[39a] See, for example: " 'The intention of Amendment No. 82 is to ensure that an applicant should always be able to require that information is supplied to him or her only in his or her preferred format, to include electronic format—which I believe is what the noble Lord, Lord Lucas, has particularly in mind. The major way of seeking to achieve that is to delete the words 'in permanent form'. But that makes no difference to the construction of the provision. If those words are deleted, the right of the applicant is to have the material provided to him in a form that is acceptable to him so far as is "reasonably practicable". Getting rid of the words "in permanent form" would not change that at all; even if they remained in the provision, the right would be the same. So there is no real difference between the Government and the noble Lord, Lord Lucas, in that respect.' The effect of that answer is that the amendment is unnecessary because the bill as drafted will ensure that an applicant can choose to have the requested information provided 'in his or her preferred format, to include electronic format': it seems that Lord Falconer believed that it had that effect because the words 'acceptable to the applicant' gave the applicant the right to specify the form in which the information was provided. It was Mr Innes's contention that the Minister's statement precisely covers the present case, but Judge Williams regarded it as inconclusive. . . . I can hardly say, in the light of the views referred to above, that my own preferred reading of section 11 (1) is unambiguously correct, and this seems to me one of the rare cases in which the *Pepper v Hart* criteria are satisfied: the Minister did

Practical application of the rule

28.1.11.1   *[New paragraph]*

The use of *Pepper v Hart* to have regard to Ministerial statements is sometimes merged into more general principles discussed elsewhere in this work[52a] allowing recourse to Parliamentary materials which shed light on the background to and policy of legislation for the purpose of applying a contextual construction.[52b]

---

in the passage which I have quoted make a clear statement directed to the very question of whether an applicant is entitled to request information in hard copy or electronic form. (I should make it clear that this is a different question from whether his answer helps on the actual issue in this case—as to which see para. 43 below.)"—*Innes v Information Commissioner* [2014] EWCA Civ 1086.

[52a] See, in particular, Ch.27.

[52b] See, for example: "35. Both Mr Tomlinson and Mr Price have sought to refer to *Hansard* to cite remarks made in the course of the Bill's passage through Parliament, relying on *Pepper v Hart* [1993] A.C. 593. I consider that it is proper to refer to the Ministerial foreword to the draft Bill, to the Joint Committee's report on the draft Bill, and to the Explanatory Notes to the Act, to identify the mischief at which it was aimed. I also consider that the parliamentary history, and in particular any respect in which the Act differs from the original draft Bill, may be highly illuminating. It is also proper to refer to statements made by the promoters of the Bill (that is to say the sponsoring minister in each House or the proposer of any successful amendment) in order to resolve a genuine ambiguity in the Act."—*Cooke v MGN Ltd* [2014] EWHC 2831 (QB); see also: "At the Committee stage in the House of Lords Lord Lucas proposed an amendment, no. 82, to the clause of the Freedom of Information bill (clause 10) which became section 11 and was in the terms eventually enacted. The amendment would have substituted for the phrase 'in permanent form or in another form acceptable to the applicant', which he said was insufficiently clear, a provision for the information to be provided 'in a form specified' by the applicant. Proposing the amendment in a debate on 17 October 2000 he said, among other things: 'If I wanted information in electronic form, as I would do, I should—we all should—be able to expect electronic information under an internet government. I do not want to be fobbed off with a paper copy that I can make no good use of. It is quite reasonable to ask for the information in electronic form.' Lord Falconer of Thoroton, for the Government, responded as follows . . . ".

Chapter 29

INTERPRETATION OF SPECIAL KINDS OF LEGISLATION

Legislation implementing international obligation

[New paragraph]   **29.1.2.2**

It is also important to remember that international Conventions are uniformly applied and interpreted in a contextual and purposive fashion.[3a] Although as in all cases the courts begin with the text of the domestic legislation itself, they will need to be satisfied that it gives accurate effect to the underlying international obligation.[3b]

European, or Europe-related, legislation

[New paragraph]   **29.1.5.1.1**

The requirement to give a purposive construction to domestic implementing legislation inevitably makes it both necessary and permissible to have regard to

---

[3a] "64. It would be wrong to read article 31 as reflecting something like the so-called 'golden rule' of statutory interpretation where one starts with the ordinary meaning of the words and then moves to other considerations only if the ordinary meaning would give rise to absurdity. That is not international law. The International Law Commission made clear in its Commentary to the draft treaty, at p 219, that, in accordance with the established international law which these provisions of VCLT codified, such a sequential mode of interpretation was not contemplated: 'The Commission, by heading the article "General rule of interpretation" in the singular and by underlining the connection between paras 1 and 2 and again between para 3 and the two previous paragraphs, intended to indicate that the application of the means of interpretation in the article would be a single combined operation."—*Moohan v The Lord Advocate* [2014] UKSC 67.

[3b] See, for example: "32. The relevant principles of interpretation where a statute or statutory instrument is enacted in order to give effect to the UK's obligations under a treaty may be summarised as follows: (1) The court must first construe the statutory enactment and if its terms are clear and unambiguous then they must be given effect to, whether or not they carry out the UK's treaty obligations—see, for example, *Salomon v Customs and Excise Commissioners* [1967] 2 QB 116, at p143 per Diplock LJ. (2) Where the terms of the statutory enactment are not clear but are reasonably capable of more than one meaning then the terms of the treaty may be considered in order to resolve the ambiguity or obscurity—see, for example, *Salomon* at p144 per Diplock LJ; *JH Rayner Ltd v Department of Trade and Industry and Others* [1990] 2 A.C. 418 at p500E per Lord Oliver; and (3) There is a prima facie presumption that the UK does not intend to legislate so as to put itself in breach of its treaty obligations so that the court will seek to construe the relevant statute or statutory instrument and the treaty in a consistent manner—see, for example, the *Salomon* case at p144; *JH Rayner* at p502E-G per Lord Oliver."—*Assuranceforeningen Gard Gjensidig v The International Oil Pollution Compensation Fund* [2014] EWHC 1394 (Comm).

background documents, such as the Explanatory Notes to primary legislation and the Explanatory Memorandum accompanying secondary legislation, to determine the social policy addressed by the legislation, even more so than in the case of legislation without a European Union connection.[13a]

Tax legislation

29.1.5.3   *[New paragraph]*

The GAAR has duly been enacted in the form of Pt 5 of the Finance Act 2013. The principal objections to the legislation as enacted are: (a) that the use of multiple layers of reasonableness entirely undermine any suggestion that the provisions will bring additional certainty to tax law; and (b) that the statutory duty for the courts to have regard to decisions of the GAAR Advisory Panel and HMRC are constitutionally objectionable, particularly in elevating a section of the tax profession who are appointed to the Panel to a position of quasi-legislative authority. The suggestion that it is abusive to exploit legislative "shortcomings"—thereby in effect making the citizen suffer by way of retrospective uncertainty for the failures of the Executive—is also particularly preposterous.

It remains to be seen how the courts will react to the GAAR and its implications. It is unlikely, however, that they will permit it to remove or undermine the fundamental principle of the law of the United Kingdom that it is for the legislature to provide for taxes in a precise way, and that in the absence of precision and certainty the courts will presume that no fiscal imposition can have been intended.[17a]

[13a] See, for example: "A national court must interpret domestic legislation, so far as possible, in the light of the wording and purpose of the Directive which it seeks to implement. This is now well settled. ... 22. It is important to note that, in order to observe the imperative that this guidance contains, the court must not only keep faith with the wording of the Directive but must have closely in mind its purpose. Since the overall purpose of the Directive is to enhance consumer protection, that overarching principle must guide interpretation of the relevant national legislation. ... 30. The 2008 Regulations can, and should, be given a purposive construction under both EU and domestic law. A purposive construction is one which eschews a narrow literal interpretation in favour of one which is consonant with the purpose of the relevant legislation, in this case, the comprehensive protection of the consumer in the event of the cancellation of the contract. As Lord Bingham observed in *R (Quintavalle) v Secretary of State for Health* [2003] 2 A.C. 687 at para 8, 'The court's task, within the permissible bounds of interpretation, is to give effect to Parliament's purpose.' Parliament's purpose was plain. As the Explanatory Memorandum makes clear, it was to ensure that all consumers should have the 'safety net' of a cooling-off period. The efficiency of that safety net would be significantly compromised if a deposit paid was not recoverable because the trader had not given written notice of a right to cancel."—*Robertson v Swift* [2014] UKSC 50.

[17a] A presumption that is clearly as vigorous as it ever was: "Coming fresh to the provision, and on a straightforward reading of Class N, I consider the more natural interpretation is that the word 'or' bears the usual disjunctive meaning that it has in common parlance. That is how I read Class N when pre-reading for the hearing. It is the way in which the Valuation Tribunal read it, without any need for especially elaborate argumentation to arrive at that conclusion. I accept that the interpretation offered by Mr Glover is a possible meaning, as a matter of English usage, but I do not think it is the most natural reading of the phrase in the context in which it appears. My first impression is reinforced by a number of contextual factors and aspects of the scheme of the Council Tax regime. I consider

Consolidation and replicating legislation

[*Add new paragraph at end of note 27*]   **29.1.8**

See also: "3. It has been said that a court 'should not routinely investigate the statutory predecessors of provisions in a consolidation statute': *R v Secretary of State for the Environment, Transport and the Regions, Ex p Spath Holme Ltd* [2001] 2 A.C. 349, 388 (Lord Bingham of Cornhill). This is not so much a rule of construction as a valuable warning against the over-ready assumption that a consolidating Act means exactly the same as the enactments which it replaces. There are, however, cases where a consolidating Act cannot be understood without reference to the state of the law as it was when it was enacted. This is one of them."—*The Manchester Ship Canal Company Ltd v United Utilities Water Plc* [2014] UKSC 40.

[*New paragraph*]   **29.1.9.1**

Although the principle of looking at previous legislation applies more widely than to straight consolidations, the more the new law deliberately changes the old in respect of substantive policy, the more cautious the courts will be about attempting to construe the new law by reference to the old.[32a]

Criminal legislation

[*Add to end of note 40*]   **29.1.13**

; see also, for example—"26. This is a statute creating a penal provision, and one of very considerable severity. The offence created is a form of homicide. To label

---

that reading the relevant phrase with the word 'or' bearing its more natural, disjunctive sense, is particularly appropriate in the context of interpretation of tax legislation such as this. It is not just officials and courts who need to know what persons are or are not exempt from liability to pay Council Tax. Ordinary members of the public may look to the legislation in order to work out whether they have a liability to pay or not, and may plan their lives and their financial affairs in the light of their own (or their advisers') straightforward reading of the provision. Although the old strictness with which tax statutes used to be read in favour of the subject is no longer taken to be the guiding presumption, in my view it remains the case that in a context in which a clearly tenable and natural reading of a provision in tax legislation favours the subject, such a reading is (subject to any clear indications to the contrary) to be preferred. The legislator is presumed to have intended to produce a result which is fair to the tax-payer and not liable to defeat his or her reasonable expectations derived from the terms of the legislation. As explained by Evans LJ in *Ingram v Inland Revenue Commissioners* [1997] 4 All E.R. 395, at 414: 'in the context of tax legislation it is necessary to consider the legal analysis with the utmost precision, so that the taxpayer shall not become liable to tax unless this is clearly and unequivocally the effect of the statutory provisions.' "—*London Borough of Harrow v Ayiku* [2012] EWHC 1200 (Admin).

[32a] "26. We would add that, unless language is obscure or unclear, it is generally neither necessary nor desirable to engage in the process of the historical examination of previous legislation to construe sections of a new statute (which POCA is) in contradistinction to a consolidating statute."—*Virgin Media Ltd, R (on the application of) v Zinga* [2014] EWCA Crim 52.

a person a criminal killer of another is of the greatest gravity. The defendant is at risk of imprisonment for a substantial term. Even if, at least in a case of inadvertent lack of insurance or venial lack of licence, a sentence of imprisonment were not to follow, the defendant would be left with a lifelong conviction for homicide which would require disclosure in the multiple situations in which one's history must be volunteered, such as the obtaining of employment, or of insurance of any kind. Nor should the personal burden or the public obloquy be underestimated; to carry the stigma of criminal conviction for killing someone else, perhaps a close relative, perhaps as in the kind of situation referred to in para 19 an innocent child, is no small thing. A penal statute falls to be construed with a degree of strictness in favour of the accused. It is undoubtedly open to Parliament to legislate to create a harsh offence or penalty, just as it is open to it to take away fundamental rights, but it is not to be assumed to have done so unless that interpretation of its statute is compelled, and compelled by the language of the statute itself. The rule of construction which applies to penal legislation, and a fortiori to legislation which carries the penalty of imprisonment, is not identical to, but is somewhat analogous to, the principle of statutory interpretation known as the principle of legality."—*R. v Hughes (Michael)* [2013] UKSC 56.

CHAPTER 31

THE LEGISLATIVE PROCESS

SECTION 1

PASSAGE OF EUROPEAN LEGISLATION

Drafting principles and practice

[New note 14a at end of first sub-paragraph (after " . . . than for their   **31.1.21**
political acceptability.")]

For judicial reference to this passage, see the speech of Lord Phillips in *Assange v The Swedish Prosecution Authority* [2012] UKSC 22.

CHAPTER 32

EUROPEAN LEGISLATION—EFFECT AND INTERPRETATION

SECTION 2

OTHER ASPECTS OF EFFECT

Extent

[Insert new note 28a at end of paragraph]   **32.2.8**

[28a] See also: "18. Secondly, in relation to the constitutional position as between the United Kingdom and Gibraltar I have concluded that Gibraltar is not to be treated as the same Member State as the UK for the purpose of Article 56 TFEU. Equally, Gibraltar is not a Member State in its own right so a restriction on trade between itself and the UK is not one on inter-Member State trade. Gibraltar is a territory with a different legal and political status to that of the UK as is made clear in Article 355(3) TFEU. However, the conclusion that Gibraltar and the UK are legally separate does not mean that a restriction on the provision of services between the two territories is without more a restriction engaging Article 56 TFEU. Whether there is such a consequence is a question of fact which focuses upon whether any of the restrictions are capable of exerting a spin-off, indirect, effect on inter-Member State trade. In the event, whilst I have expressed scepticisms as to whether such an effect could in fact arise, it has not been necessary to form a decided conclusion on this. . . . 231. The extent to which EU law is therefore applicable to any one or more of the foreign territories associated with Member States is not uniform. It is common ground in this case that the relationship between Gibraltar and the United Kingdom is governed by Article 355(3). From this the following may be deduced. First, Gibraltar is a territory within Europe. Secondly, it is a territory for whose external relations the United Kingdom is responsible. Thirdly, in consequence the provisions of the Treaty apply to Gibraltar. 232. It is in my view implicit in Article 355(3) that Gibraltar does not constitute the same Member State that assumes responsibility for it. Were it otherwise there would be no need to have a treaty provision governing the responsibility of the third territory for adherence to EU law; it would have been subject to the law upon the basis that it was part of 'the' relevant Member State. 233. This conclusion was reflected in Declaration 55 to the Final Act of the Intergovernmental Conference which adopted the Treaty of Lisbon (signed on 13th December 2007). The Declaration which was signed by the Kingdom of Spain and United Kingdom provides: 'The Treaties apply to Gibraltar as a European territory for whose external relations a Member State is responsible. This shall not imply changes in the respective positions of the Member States concerned'. . . . 267. There are two final observations I would make. First, although I have held that the relationship between Gibraltar and the UK is not intra-Member State, even if I had held that it was a purely internal matter operating within a single Member State it would still, at least in theory, have been open to the Claimant to argue that there were spill-over or indirect effects on trade between Member States. The case law shows that the simple fact that the parties are in one Member State, and that this is where

the restriction primarily bites, is not conclusive. Ultimately, whether this is so or not is a question of fact, as the authorities that I have cited above demonstrate. Secondly, for the avoidance of doubt my conclusions have been arrived at in the context of the relationship between the UK and Gibraltar. I have not therefore addressed the position as between Gibraltar and other Member States."—*Gibraltar Betting & Gaming Association Ltd v The Secretary of State for Culture, Media & Sport the Gambling Commission* [2014] EWHC 3236 (Admin).

Section 5

Interpretation

Introduction

32.5.1   *[New note 63a at end of first sub-paragraph (after " . . . earlier in this work.")]*

For judicial approbation of this passage, see the speech of Lord Phillips in *Assange v The Swedish Prosecution Authority* [2012] UKSC 22.

Consistency of construction

32.5.5   *[Insert at end of note 78]*

; see also—"The law can be summarised shortly. All EU law instruments must be construed teleologically or purposively and the purpose behind a measure is identifiable, in the first, instance, from the recitals to the measure in issue. In Case 14/82 *Von Colson* [1984] E.C.R. 1891 at paragraph [26] the Court held that the Member States were under a duty to achieve the "result envisaged by the directive" and that this obligation extended to all organs of the State including its judicial emanations. In Case C106/89 *Marleasing* [1990] E.C.R. I-4153 the Court held that in the light of this a ' . . . national court called upon to interpret [national law] is required to do so, as far as possible, in the light of the wording and the purpose of the directive' (paragraph [8]). In that case the Court identified the purpose of the directive from the preamble (cf paragraph [12]). Where there is ambiguity a Court may also look to the travaux preparatoires. In this case no one has suggested that the recitals do not provide an ample exposition of the purpose or that any further elucidation would be obtained from reviewing the pre-legislative travaux. I did conduct an informal review of the travaux but found nothing which added to that which was set out in the recitals."—*UK Power Networks Services (Contracting) Ltd, R (on the Application of) v The Gas and Electricity Markets Authority* [2014] EWHC 3678 (Admin); see also—"47. As is well known, the approach of the ECJ/CJEU to interpretation is teleological: the search is for an interpretation that gives effect to the objectives of the Directive. These include (a) uniformity in the application of EU law (b) 'effectiveness' or 'effet utile' and (c) the achievement of the aims of the Directive, as expressed in its recitals, being to enable, facilitate and reduce the complexity of cross-border mergers. 48. Thus, literal meaning may have to yield to a teleological or purposive approach: see again *Re Itaú* at paragraph 5. Even if the wording in EU legislation may, as a matter of purely semantic analysis, seem clear, it is still necessary to refer to the spirit, general scheme and the context of the provision or the practicalities of its operation: see Vaughan and Robertson, 'Law of the European Union' at 3[81]; and *Gebrueder Knauf Westdeutsche Gipswerke v Hauptzollamt Hamburg-Jonas* [1980] E.C.R. 1183 at para 5.49. Further, the text of a provision of EU legislation comprises all authentic versions expressed in the official EU languages: preference is not to be given to any one version, and the search is for a meaning best consonant with all the versions: see Vaughan and Robertson, 'Law of the European Union' at 3[82]; and *Jany and Others v Staatssecretaris van Justitie* [2001] E.C.R. 1-8615 at para 47. Care must be taken to identify an autonomous meaning where appropriate, rather than any specific domestic meaning."—*Olympus UK Ltd* [2014] EWHC 1350 (Ch).

[New paragraph]   **32.5.7A**

Despite being a fundamental principle of the European Union's comity, it should always be remembered that, so far as the courts of the United Kingdom are concerned, *Marleasing* is a principle of statutory interpretation, and there are limits beyond which that process cannot go without doing too much violence to the statutory language and structure to be capable of being considered interpretation at all. It is open to the domestic courts, if necessary, to depart from the legislative intent of United Kingdom legislation in order to give effect to the primacy of European Union law in accordance with the European Communities Act 1972,[83a] but the application of the *Marleasing* rule is a less powerful process and cannot be used to resolve fundamental incompatibilities.[83b] Subject to that, however, the courts will allow themselves greater latitude in relation to the

---

[83a] See Ch.32:4 and the *Factortame* litigation referred to there.

[83b] See, for example: "It is clear that, prior to the amendments to the CDPA pursuant to the 2003 Regulations, section 72(1) provided a defence to infringement of copyright by a restricted act within section 19(3) but not to infringement of copyright by a restricted act within section 20. It is also clear from the contemporaneous documents to which Mr Mellor referred (the Government's 2002 consultation paper on the implementation of the Copyright Directive, the Draft Regulatory Impact Assessment annexed to it, the analysis of responses to the consultation, including the Government's conclusions, the transposition note which accompanied the 2003 Regulations, and the Explanatory Note at the end of the 2003 Regulations) that the Government intended to comply with, and fully to implement, the Copyright Directive. It is also clear that, at the time the 2003 Regulations were made and the CDPA was amended to give effect to them, the Government did not appreciate that 'the communication to the public of the work' in the amended section 20 included the 'showing or playing in public of a broadcast' within section 72(1). In the language of Mr Mellor's oral submissions, the Government did not understand that the act of receiving a broadcast and showing it on a television to a public audience that had not paid for admission fell within the restricted act of communication to the public. 51. I do not agree with Mr Mellor, however, that it is therefore in accordance with the Marleasing principle to interpret section 72(1)(c) as implicitly limited to restricted acts within section 19(3) on the ground that such an interpretation would give effect to both the Government's intention to comply with the Copyright Directive and also to the Government's belief that section 72(1)(c) would continue to be limited to restricted acts within section 19(3) as before. I consider that such a conforming interpretation would go beyond the principles of legitimate statutory interpretation."—*Football Association Premier League Ltd v QC Leisure* [2012] EWCA Civ 1708.

statutory text when applying a conforming construction under the *Marleasing* rule than when ordinarily applying a purposive construction.[83c]

32.5.7B   *[New paragraph]*

Although the *Marleasing* process is one of interpretation, the courts may in an appropriate case express the result of the application of a conforming construction under the rule as a notional textual amendment of the Act.[83d] The process, is, however, purely notional, and the actual text of the domestic legislation remains unaffected.

[83c] See, for example: "(i) The need for a purposive construction of Article 13(2) and Regulation 18(4): It is clear that, in the case of legislation implementing EU law, there is a greater flexibility in applying a purposive construction: see, for example, Lord Oliver in *Pickstone v Freemans plc* [1989] 1 A.C. 66 at 126 and *Litster v Forth Dry Dock and Engineering Co Ltd* [1990] 1 A.C. 546 at 576–577. Indeed, there is a duty to construe such implementing legislation, so far as possible, to give effect to the objective of the European legislation the national legislation was designed to implement, and to do so by a more robust approach to the adoption of a strained construction than in cases where no question of Community law is involved. In *Russell v TransOcean International Resources Ltd* [2011] UKSC 57 at [22], Lord Hope DPSC stated that, because of this duty, the terms of the implementing legislation "are of secondary importance" to the terms of the Directive, although they are relevant as they set out the domestic rules that must be complied with in conformity with the obligations in the Directive, in that case the Working Time Directive 2003/88."—*R. (on the application of Hemming (t/a Simply Pleasure Ltd)) v Westminster City Council* [2013] EWCA Civ 591.

[83d] See, for example: "Section 151(8) in fact demands that two pre-conditions be fulfilled before the insurer has the right to an indemnity from the insured. It has to be shown that the insured "caused or permitted[70] the use of the vehicle" and that the use of the vehicle "gave rise to the liability". So I think it cannot be against the fundamental principle of section 151(8) to require further conditions be fulfilled in certain limited circumstances before the insurer can exercise the right (to whatever extent may seem proportionate) against an insured passenger victim. Accordingly, I would prefer the interpretation advanced by the insurers and the SST. I would interpret section 151(8)(b) as notionally including the words added in bold italics: "Where an insurer becomes liable under this section to pay an amount in respect of a liability of a person who is not insured in a policy . . . he is entitled to recover the amount from . . . any person who— . . . (b) caused or permitted the use of the vehicle which gave rise to the liability, *save that where the person insured by the policy may be entitled to the benefit of any judgment to which this section refers, any recovery by the insurer in respect of that judgment must be proportionate and determined on the basis of the circumstances of the case*"."—*Churchill Insurance Company Ltd v Fitzgerald & Wilkinson* [2012] EWCA Civ 1166.

APPENDICES

EXTRACTS AND APPENDIX

CHURCH MEASURES

APPENDIX 3 TO THE 25TH REPORT OF THE HOUSE OF LORDS SELECT COMMITTEE ON MERITS OF STATUTORY INSTRUMENTS SESSION 2003–04

Letter from Stephen Slack, Chief Legal Adviser to the Archbishop's Council, to the Clerk

I am writing in connection with the new Select Committee on the Merits of Statutory Instruments referred to in Statutory Instrument Practice Circulars Nos 2 (04) and 3 (04).

I note that the terms of reference of the Merits Committee as recorded in the House of Lords motion of 17th December 2003 are apparently all embracing in terms of the instruments which the Committee will consider, subject only to a small number of specified exceptions.

As you will doubtless know, Measures of the General Synod (and of its predecessor the Church Assembly), which of course have statutory force under the Church of England Assembly (Powers) Act 1919, sometimes confer power upon the Synod or other Church bodies to make subordinate legislation to which the Statutory Instruments Act 1946 is applied.

The most frequently made statutory instruments are those relating to different types of fees under the Ecclesiastical Fees Measure 1986. (The 2004 orders under that Measure will be laid later this month after their forthcoming consideration by the General Synod.) But the same procedure is used in a range of other contexts as well. Thus, for example, since 2000 the General Synod has passed the Faculty Jurisdiction Rules 2000, the Faculty Jurisdiction (Care of Places of Worship) Rules 2000, the Parsonages Measure Rules 2000, the National Institutions Measure 1998 (Amendment) Resolution 2001 and the Payments to the Churches Conservation Trust Order 2003. Future examples will include Rules made under the Clergy Discipline Measure 2003 and the Care of Cathedrals Measures.

Against this background, you will appreciate that having the Church's statutory instruments subject to scrutiny by the Merits Committee in accordance with the arrangements set out in the recent Circulars would raise a number of issues for us, not least in terms of the implications from the constitutional point of view of legislation of the Church of England being subjected to scrutiny in terms of its policy objectives.

I should accordingly be grateful if you could please clarify whether or not is intended that the new arrangements should in fact apply to statutory instruments made under the authority of Measures of the Church of England. If it is intended that they should, I think we shall wish to address further arguments to your Committee in that connection.

I am about to leave the office for a few days in order to attend the forthcoming group of sessions of the General Synod in York but should be very happy to discuss this matter on my return if that would be helpful.

7 July 2004

Letter from the Clerk to Stephen Slack, Chief Legal Adviser to the Archbishop's Council

Thank you for your letter of 7 July, the content of which we have discussed over the telephone and I have discussed with Robert Wellen.

The remit of the Merits Committee requires it, subject to certain exemptions, "to consider every instrument which is laid before each House of Parliament and upon which proceedings may be or might have been taken in either House of Parliament, in pursuance of an Act of Parliament ... ". Given the absence of a specific exemption, in my view, subordinate legislation made under the Church of England Assembly (Powers) Act 1919 ("the 1919 Act") which is subject to either the affirmative or negative procedure falls within the terms of reference of the Merits Committee. This contrasts with the position with regard to the Joint Committee on Statutory Instruments, the terms of reference of which specifically excludes consideration of such instruments.

My understanding is, therefore, that you are required to produce an explanatory memorandum (EM) in respect of instruments made under the 1919 Act and that they will be considered by the Merits Committee.

However, as I mentioned on the telephone, the terms of reference of the Committee are to be reviewed after the end of the session. It would be of assistance to the Merits Committee therefore, on first consideration of a 1919 Act instrument (that is, at its meeting on Tuesday 7 September), if you were to write to the Committee to explain why, in your view, consideration of 1919 Act instruments by the Merits Committee would raise issues for the Archbishops' Council.

28 July 2004

Letter from Stephen Slack, Chief Legal Adviser to the Archbishop's Council, to the Clerk

I note your view that subordinate legislation made under the Church of England Assembly (Powers) Act 1919 ('the Enabling Act) and subject to the affirmative or negative resolution procedure currently falls within the terms of reference of the Merits Committee. However, having had more opportunity to consider the matter further since I wrote my earlier letter and to discuss the matter with Sir Anthony Hammond KCB QC (who as Standing Counsel to the General Synod is responsible for drafting our Measures), I wonder with respect whether that is in fact the case.

The terms of reference of the Merits Committee of course extend to instruments "upon which proceedings may or might have been taken in either House of Parliament, in pursuance of an Act of Parliament". As you point out, in that respect they differ from the terms of reference of the Joint Committee on Statutory Instruments ('JCSI'), which include an additional limb also bringing within the scope of the JCSI "every general statutory instrument not within the foregoing classes . . . not including measures under the Church of England Assembly (Powers) Act 1919 and instruments made under such measures". (The reference to Measures themselves presumably reflects the view that Measures themselves represent a form of delegated legislation: see, for example, the advice of the then Counsel to the Speaker to that effect contained in the Report of the Joint Committee on Delegated Legislation (1971–1 HL, 184, HC 475, x).)

It seems to me that the wording of the terms of reference of the JCSI properly reflects the fact that instruments made under Measures would not fall within the first class of instruments they mention since such instruments are not ones "upon which proceedings may or might have been taken . . . in pursuance of an Act of Parliament": any proceedings would be taken under the authority of the Measure which conferred the power under which the instrument in question was made. (That this is the correct analysis is supported by the Second Special Report of the Commons Statutory Instruments Committee (HC 7–v (1953–54).) It follows, I suggest, that even though there is no express exclusion of instruments made under Measures from the terms of reference of the Merits Committee, they nonetheless do not embrace such instruments.

I hope that the Committee will feel able to agree with this analysis. However, lest it does not do so, or is minded to propose an amendment to its terms of reference so that they include instruments made under Measures, I think it might assist if I commented on the wider issue of the appropriateness of their scrutiny by the Merits Committee.

The Enabling Act of course conceded the principle of self-governance in legislative matters to the Church, subject to certain safeguards centred on a process of scrutiny by the Ecclesiastical Committee of Parliament and the need for an affirmative resolution of both Houses. In particular, under s.3(3) of the

Enabling Act the role of the Ecclesiastical Committee is to consider a Measure and then to "draft a report thereon to Parliament stating the nature and legal effect of the measure and its views as to the expediency thereof, especially with relation to the constitutional rights of all His Majesty's subject". As part of that process it considers the appropriateness of any powers to make delegated legislation. (See the Minutes of the Proceedings of the Ecclesiastical Committee, Vol I, 379–382.)

The Ecclesiastical Committee has seen its responsibilities under s.3 of the Enabling Act as extending well beyond making technical legal points (such as drawing attention to drafting defects) into what might be seen as policy matters. However, my understanding is that it has taken the line that there are some contexts in which it would be inappropriate for it to take a view on the merits, on the ground that the matters in question are best left for the Church to determine. These include matters of doctrine and liturgy (except so far as they impinge on the Church's legal position as the Established Church) and matters of the Church's own internal administration. I believe that the Ecclesiastical Committee has been correct to adopt this approach: if ever the Court were called on to consider the effect of s.3 of the Enabling Act, I think it would take the view (not least in the light of its legislative history) that the Committee should not operate as a kind of select committee inquiring into the general merits of a Measure or duplicate the General Synod's own detailed consideration of it. Moreover, it can be argued that the matters to be taken into account by the Ecclesiastical Committee should be ones relevant to a Measure's legal effect, rather than to its implications for the Church of England viewed purely as a religious body or its members as such (for example, on questions of doctrine and liturgy).

When the extent to which the Ecclesiastical Committee can properly address the merits of Church of England Measures is limited in the way I have described, it would seem open to question in principle whether the Merits Committee should have a more wide-ranging role in relation to the merits of statutory instruments made under such Measures. Support for this view may be found in the deliberate exclusion of Church of Measures and instruments made under them from the scope of the JCSI: the report of the Joint Committee on Delegated Legislation which led to its creation reported, after explaining the process of scrutiny by the Ecclesiastical Committee and approval by both Houses, that "the Committee's inquiries have not elicited any suggestion that improvements need to be made in the procedures or practice by which Parliament exercises control over [this kind] of instrument". In the light of that conclusion, for statutory instruments made under Measures to be subject to scrutiny as regards their policy content when they are exempt from scrutiny as to their form would not only be anomalous but would also seem to require some justification.

Finally, I understand the underlying concern behind the establishment of the Merits Committee to be the lack of effective scrutiny of statutory instruments.

However, delegated legislation made under Measures in the form of statutory instruments is already subject to scrutiny under the Church's own internal legislative procedures. The Standing Orders of the General Synod, made under powers conferred by the Synodical Government Measure 1969, require the approval of the Synod for such legislation and contain provisions enabling any member to require such legislation be debated and to propose amendments to it. It is not uncommon for advantage to be taken of those provisions, with amendments being proposed and debated before approval is finally given to an instrument. Indeed, sometimes the Synod declines to approve then (as was the case at its July group of sessions, for example, when the Synod rejected the Legal Officers (Annual Fees) Order because of reservations about the policy it had adopted as regards the increase in the retainer paid to diocesan registrars).

In conclusion, I hope the Committee will feel able to agree, as part of its review of its terms of reference, that as currently drafted its terms of reference do not extend to instruments made under Measures and that they should not be amended so as to do so. If the Committee requires any further information in order to be able to consider the matter, however, please do not hesitate to let me know.

3 September 2004

Letter from the Clerk to Stephen Slack, Chief Legal Adviser to the Archbishop's Council

Thank you for your letter of 3 September, which was put before the Merits of Statutory Instruments Committee at its meeting on 14 September. The Committee gave preliminary consideration to the issues raised in your letter but have asked for further information before reaching a view.

During the Committee's deliberations, a question was raised about the application of the Statutory Instruments Act 1946 to the three instruments currently before House, and, in particular, about the reasons for the Church choosing to apply a procedure—the negative resolution procedure—which envisages the possibility of parliamentary scrutiny and intervention. The Committee would welcome your views on this point.

The Committee will meet again on Tuesday 12 October. It would be most helpful if you were able to provide to response to this letter by Wednesday 6 October. Please do not hesitate to let me know if this causes you any difficulties.

29 September 2004

Letter from Stephen Slack, Chief Legal Adviser to the Archbishop's Council, to the Clerk

The reason that the negative or affirmative procedure is applied to instruments made under Measures is that the Standing Orders of the General Synod provide that

" . . . no Measure . . . shall contain any provision empowering an authority to make a subordinate instrument having the force of law of general, as distinct from local, application, unless it also provides . . . that such instrument (not being a scheme or part of a scheme to be approved by Her Majesty in Council), if it affects the legal rights of any person, shall be laid before both Houses of Parliament and be subject to approval or annulment in pursuance of a resolution of either House as may be determined by that Measure".

In the time available I have not been able fully to research the origin of this provision, save to establish that a provision broadly to this effect has been included in the Standing Orders of the General Synod since its creation in 1970.

However, given the way that it is expressed, I believe that it is intended to prevent a position arising in which instruments made under Measures containing provisions affecting peoples' rights which, had they been contained in a Measure, would have been subject to Parliamentary scrutiny escape such scrutiny. Such a situation would seem to be inconsistent with the spirit of the Church of England Assembly (Powers) Act 1919 and would, no doubt, be unwelcome to both the Ecclesiastical Committee and Parliament. (Indeed, its undesirability was referred to in the Report of a Sub-committee of the Ecclesiastical Committee appointed to consider delegated legislation under Church Assembly Measures, which pointed out that instruments made under Measures "might 'affect the rights of all His Majesty's subjects' but would nevertheless escape the scrutiny of the Ecclesiastical Committee and the confirmation by Parliament for which the Act provides".)

On this basis, I would argue that subjecting instruments made under Measures to the affirmative or negative resolution procedure does not imply an acceptance of the same degree of Parliamentary scrutiny as that to which other instruments placed before Parliament are subject. Rather, the intended purpose of doing so is to give Parliament the same ability to reject instruments affecting peoples' rights as it has to reject Measures themselves. And if, as I explained in my previous letter, the Ecclesiastical Committee itself appears to accept that there are limits on the extent to which it can and should review the merits of a Measure in order to assist Parliament in deciding whether or not to approve it, it seems to me that it would be inappropriate for the Merits Committee to have a wider remit in relation to instruments made under Measures, which enabled it to examine the merits of such instruments generally.

I hope this is of assistance to the Committee.

11 October 2004

Letter from the Clerk to Stephen Slack, Chief Legal Adviser to the Archbishop's Council

At its meeting yesterday, the Merits Committee considered whether instruments made under Measures of the General Synod fell within its terms of reference and concluded that they did. The Committee therefore considered the three instruments before it and determined that they should not be reported to the House. I enclose a copy of the Committee's report. The instruments appear in the (lengthy) list of instruments not reported (Appendix 1).

The Chairman of the Merits Committee, Lord Hunt of Kings Heath, has written to the Chairman of the Procedure Committee, Lord Brabazon of Tara, to inform him of the Merits Committee's view.

14 October 2004

PASSAGE OF NON-PUBLIC BILLS
HYBRID BILLS
EXTRACT FROM THE JUDGMENT IN *HS2 ACTION ALLIANCE LTD, R (ON THE APPLICATION OF) v THE SECRETARY OF STATE FOR TRANSPORT* ([2014] UKSC 3)

57. It may be helpful at the outset to explain what is meant by hybrid bill procedure. A hybrid bill shares certain characteristics of a public bill and a private bill. The Speaker has defined a hybrid bill as "a public bill which affects a particular private interest in a manner different from the private interests of other persons or bodies of the same category or class" (Hansard (HC Debates), 10 December 1962, col 45). This hybrid character influences the Parliamentary procedure: a hybrid bill proceeds as a public bill, with a second reading, committee report and third reading, but with an additional select committee stage after the second reading in each House, at which objectors whose interests are directly and specifically affected by the bill (including local authorities) may petition against the bill and be heard. Parliamentary standing orders make provision for those persons who have standing to lodge a petition.

58. It is for Parliament and not the Government to determine the Parliamentary procedure for a hybrid bill laid before it. It is however a matter of agreement between the parties that, in the case of the hybrid bill for Phase 1 of HS2, the principle of the bill will be set upon the bill's receiving a second reading following debate, subject to the Government whip, in the House of Commons. It is expected that the principle of the bill will extend to a high speed rail line running between London, Birmingham and the West Midlands, with its central London terminus at Euston and a link to HS1 (ie the Channel Tunnel Rail Link). It is also common ground that the established convention is that a select committee for a hybrid bill cannot hear petitions which seek to challenge the principle of the bill, unless instructed to do so by the House at second reading (Erskine May's Treatise on the Law, Privileges, Proceedings and Usage of Parliament, 24th ed (2011), ed Jack, p 656). Under the Parliamentary procedures as currently envisaged by the Government, matters that go to the principle of the bill will not be considered by the select committee. Such matters would be expected to include the business case for HS2, alternatives to the high speed rail

project and alternative routes for Phase 1. The principle of the bill could in theory be re-opened at third reading, but that debate also will be subject to the Government whip.

The relevant standing orders

59. In order to understand the arguments, it is also necessary to note the relevant Parliamentary standing orders ("SOs"). SO 27A for Private Business requires that a bill authorising the carrying out of works the nature and extent of which are specified in the bill must be accompanied by an environmental statement, which must be available for inspection and for sale at a reasonable price. The environmental statement must contain the information required by the Town and Country Planning (Environmental Impact Assessment) Regulations 2011 (SI 2011/1824), "the 2011 Regulations"), which transpose the requirements of the EIA Directive, so far as affecting applications for planning permission, into English law.

60. SO 224A, which was introduced in June 2013 after the hearing of the appeal in the Court of Appeal, requires that upon the deposit of the bill a notice must be published stating that any person who wishes to make comments on the environmental statement should send those comments to the minister responsible for the bill. The minister must publish and deposit the comments received, and submit them to an independent assessor appointed by the Examiner of Petitions for Private Bills. The assessor is then to prepare a report summarising the issues raised by those comments. The report must be submitted to the House at least 14 days prior to second reading. At third reading the minister must set out the main reasons and considerations upon which Parliament is invited to consent to the project and the main measures to avoid, reduce and if possible offset the project's major adverse effects. A written statement must be laid before the House not less than seven days before third reading. The House of Lords has made corresponding arrangements under SO 83A.

Whips

61. Finally, by way of introduction, it is necessary to consider the role of Government whips. In that regard, although the argument on behalf of the appellants was largely concerned with the implications, for the purposes of assessing compliance with the EIA Directive, of the fact that votes on the bill are intended to be subject to the Government whip, the court was not provided with any authoritative account of how the whip operates.

62. In general terms, the Government whips are ministers responsible for fitting the Government's programme of business into the time available during the session. The Opposition parties also have whips, who are members of either House, appointed by their party in Parliament to help organise their party's contribution to Parliamentary business. The term is derived from hunting: a

whipper-in is a huntsman's assistant, who drives straying hounds back to the pack using a whip. One of the whips' duties is to see that their parties are as fully represented as possible at important votes or "divisions", and, in the Commons, to arrange "pairs" for members who wish to be absent (a "pair" being a member of the opposite party who also wishes to be absent). Each week they send a circular to their Members of Parliament or peers, detailing the forthcoming Parliamentary business. Items underlined once are considered routine and attendance is optional. Those underlined twice are more important and attendance is expected unless a "pair" has been arranged. Items underlined three times, such as second readings of significant bills, are highly important. The failure of Government backbenchers to attend a vote with a three-line whip, or their voting contrary to Government policy on such an occasion, may have disadvantageous consequences for them within their party, including in extreme circumstances the possibility of suspension from the Parliamentary party. In that event the member keeps his seat but sits as an independent until the whip is restored.

63. In practice, Members of Parliament have to consider a range of factors besides the guidance of the whips. For example, in relation to controversial developments affecting their constituencies, Members of Parliament have to consider the views of their constituents: if they fail to do so, they may lose their constituents' support, and may in consequence be liable to lose their seat at the next election.

64. Although Government backbenchers generally support Government policies, failures to vote in accordance with the whip are not infrequent. One recent study found that Members of Parliament on the Government benches had voted against the whip in 43% of divisions during the first 18 months of the current Government: P Cowley and M Stuart, "A Coalition with Two Wobbly Wings: Backbench Dissent in the House of Commons", (2012) Political Insight, 3, pp 8–11. It also has to be borne in mind that the apprehension of backbench dissent may result in changes to proposed legislation, so as to ensure that the Government will not be defeated. A study of the Government elected in 2001 carried out by Professor Philip Cowley of the University of Nottingham, for example, concluded that the fact that it had never suffered a defeat on a whipped vote could "hardly be seen as evidence of parliamentary impotence ... From the very beginning, the 2001 Parliament saw the Government give ground to its backbench critics on measure after measure, including on almost all major policy initiatives": Cowley, *The Rebels: How Blair Mislaid His Majority* (2005), pp 242-243. The same study commented that to focus on the weakness of Members of Parliament and the disciplinary power of the whips was "a quite monumental failure to understand the realities of parliamentary life" (op cit, p 48).

65. In some circumstances, it may in any event be impractical for the Government to proceed with a project without the support of the Opposition, as well as that of its own backbenchers. That may be the position, for example,

where the period of time over which substantial Government resources require to be committed will extend beyond the Parliament during which the necessary legislation is enacted. In such a situation, there may be little purpose in obtaining Parliamentary approval for a project unless there is confidence that a future government, even if of a different party, will continue to support the project as so approved. Whether the HS2 project might be in that position, as has been suggested in public debate on the issue, was not addressed in the submissions.

66. In relation to voting in Parliament, it is also relevant to note the convention that members of the Government do not vote against Government legislation. If they do so, they are generally expected to resign, failing which they may be dismissed. Their loss of office does not affect their position as Members of Parliament.

LEGISLATIVE DRAFTING—SPECIFIC ISSUES

GENDER NEUTRAL DRAFTING

MINISTER'S REPLY TO HOUSE OF LORDS DEBATE DECEMBER 12, 2013[1]

"For many years parliamentary counsel, who draft legislation, relied on Section 6 of the Interpretation Act 1978, to which my noble and learned friend Lord Mackay of Clashfern and the noble and learned Lord, Lord Scott of Foscote, referred. That provision says that words referring to the masculine gender include the feminine, and vice versa. In practice, this means that male pronouns such as 'he' were used in contexts where a reference to women and men was intended. This indeed aided brevity, but many people believed that the practice tended to reinforce historical gender stereotypes. The noble Lord, Lord Quirk, gave your Lordships some good examples of that.

The policy of gender-neutral language in legislation was announced by the previous Government in a Written Statement on 8 March 2007, as the noble Lord, Lord Kennedy of Southwark, said. Parliamentary counsel were asked to use,

> 'gender-neutral drafting so far as it is practicable, at no more than a reasonable cost to brevity or intelligibility'.—[*Official Report*, Commons, 8/3/07; col. 146WS.]

However, I reassure the noble and learned Lord, Lord Scott, that we are not abandoning the Interpretation Act. The 1978 Act is still needed for amendments to old legislation that predates the move to gender-neutral drafting. The noble Lord, Lord Kennedy of Southwark, referred to that. Parliamentary counsel sometimes still use gender-specific pronouns when amending old legislation to ensure that it remains coherent. The 1978 Act enables masculine or feminine words to be used in legislation to cover both genders but does not contain drafting guidance about how to draft.

---

[1] HL Deb 12.12.13 cc.1004–1016.

Even before the move to gender-neutral drafting in 2007, there was no requirement to use gender-specific pronouns. There are plenty of examples of old provisions that were drafted in gender-neutral terms and without reliance on the 1978 Act. Interestingly, the 1978 Act was a consolidation and may be traced back to legislation first enacted in 1850. I know that the noble and learned Lord, Lord Scott of Foscote, referred to the 1978 Act as not being ancient, but 1850, while it may not be very ancient, is quite a long time ago.

The move to gender-neutral drafting brought us in line with other jurisdictions which use the English language, where it had been the norm for many years: Ireland, New Zealand, Canada, parts of Australia and the United States of America, as well as the three devolved legislatures. The noble Lord, Lord Kennedy of Southwark, included South Africa in that list. With the change to gender-neutral drafting, a range of drafting styles was developed: for example, omitting the pronoun, repeating the noun, replacing the noun with a letter such as the letter P, using defined terms or using 'he' or 'she', and so on. Parliamentary counsel have tried to simplify drafting so that it is not ambiguous or too lengthy.

In places, the move caused drafters to reword propositions so that they indeed became shorter and clearer. For example, 'the Secretary of State may, if he thinks fit' could become simply, 'the Secretary of State may'. Before the change, the drafting may have said, 'A person commits an offence if he drops litter in a public place', but now it could be simplified to, 'A person who drops litter in a public place commits an offence'. However, we recognise that there are some techniques that people find easier to follow than others, and I have much sympathy with people who do not like techniques such as the use of letters—'P' and so on—to identify different people.

I hope that your Lordships will be pleased to note that the Office of the Parliamentary Counsel has agreed to revise its drafting guidance to recommend that the approach of using letters to identify people is used sparingly, although it may sometimes be a useful way to distinguish between several people. It will also be considering whether any other adjustments could usefully be made in light of the helpful feedback from this debate.

Etymologists may disagree but the guidance from parliamentary counsel provides that some terms are to be treated as gender-neutral. These include 'testator', 'manager' and 'actor', although they have female equivalents. There are also some terms that have always been gender-neutral—for example, Secretary of State and Prime Minister.

Gender-specific pronouns are still sometimes used in legislation that amends older legislation, as it is important for the amended Act to remain coherent. For example, if there is a list of conditions each of which begins with 'he', it would be confusing to start a new condition starting with 'the person'.

The guidance also recognises that there must be some flexibility and that there will be some Acts where only gender-specific drafting can be usefully applied. In a case where a person has to be of a particular gender—male or female—gender-neutral drafting does not require drafters to avoid referring to the gender. I think your Lordships would agree that that would be the case for legislation about maternity.

I turn to the specific points raised by the noble and learned Lord, Lord Scott of Foscote, in his detailed account of various provisions in subordinate legislation. I hope that he will forgive me if I do not engage in what I would call the intricacies of what he has quite rightly outlined, but I reassure noble Lords that the Government remain committed to producing high-quality legislation that is clear, accessible and free from ambiguity. We believe that gender-neutral drafting is perfectly compatible with that objective. It ensures that our law is expressed in a way that clearly covers all citizens without requiring people to consult Section 6 of the Interpretation Act 1978.

Most of the examples that were mentioned concern the use of 'they' as the third person singular pronoun. Although some regard this usage as grammatically incorrect, it reflects common usage, as my noble and learned friend Lord Mackay of Clashfern said with regard to the brief from the Library, and is well precedented in literature over the centuries. However, the noble Lord, Lord Quirk, referred to the risks of using the word 'they' in the singular form. This is noted in the parliamentary counsel's drafting guidance, and care obviously needs to be taken when drafting any legislation to ensure that it is not ambiguous.

I turn to the Good Law initiative, which the First Parliamentary Counsel is spearheading. This initiative, about which I have spoken before in your Lordships' House, aims to improve drafting, reduce complexity and make the law more accessible, and I believe that these are the objectives that we all seek. The parliamentary counsel's initial report aspires to good law, which is defined as necessary, effective, clear, accessible, coherent and, if I am allowed, I would like to add my noble and learned friend Lord Mackay's word 'lucid'. This is a sentiment that I very much hope we share across all sides of the House. With that in mind, the Government acknowledge that the use of gender-neutral drafting must result in legislation that is effective, clear and accessible."

INTERPRETATION ACT 1978 s.7
PRESUMPTIONS OF SERVICE[1]

Freetown v Assethold Ltd [2012] EWCA Civ 1657

Extract from the judgment of Lord Justice Rix

10   This court's decision in 2003 in *Webber v. Railtrack* was, and remains, the latest in a line of jurisprudence on the meaning of "sending it through the post in a registered letter" in section 23(1) of the LTA 1927. Some but by no means all of that jurisprudence also considers the interrelationship of that provision with section 7 of the Interpretation Act 1927.

11   The issue in Webber arose in the following way. A landlord sent his tenant notices pursuant to section 25 of the Landlord and Tenant Act 1954 ("LTA 1954"), to inform him that he would oppose the grant of new tenancies. Such a notice had to be sent not less than six months before the specified date of termination, here 22 January 2002. The notices were posted by recorded delivery on 20 July 2001, received on 23 July, and responded to on 24 July to the effect that the tenant was unwilling to give up possession. Subsequently the tenant sought a declaration that the landlord's notices had been served out of time because received within the six month period. So the question whether service was effected by posting or by receipt was again critical. Section 66(4) of the LTA 1954 applied section 23 of the LTA 1927 to the question. This court held that section 7 of the Interpretation Act was excluded, that service was effected by posting by recorded delivery, and that such an interpretation was compatible with article 6 of the European Convention on Human Rights (ECHR), as well as to article 1 of its First Protocol.

12   The essence of the reasoning was that the matter had been decided by the weight of authority, and particularly by the decision in this court in *Galinski v. McHugh* (1988) 57 P&CR 359 : section 23 afforded three primary, alternative, methods of service, each of which was equally effective when performed. It followed that posting by registered post was effective at the time the registered letter was put into the post, and that section 7 of the Interpretation Act was necessarily excluded.

---

[1] See new paragraph 22.1.12.2 above.

13   In *Galinski*, Slade LJ, delivering the judgment of the court, had said (at 365):

"In our judgment, the object of . . . [section 23(1)] . . . is not to protect the person upon whom the right to receive the notice is conferred by other statutory provisions. On the contrary, section 23(1) is intended to assist the person who is obliged to serve the notice, by offering him choices of mode of service which will be deemed to be valid service, even if in the event the intended recipient does not in fact receive it."

In *Webber*, Peter Gibson LJ cited that passage and observed:

"[22] The general proposition laid down by this court in that case was that the purpose of section 23 is not to protect the addressee of the notice, but to assist the server of the notice by offering him choices as to how to effect service in ways which will be deemed to be good service, even if the notice is never received by the intended recipient. That, as it appears to me, was a necessary part of the reasoning of the decision of this court. It is a part which was detached and abstracted from the specific peculiarities of the particular case which gave rise to the decision. Accordingly, in my judgment, that was ratio and binding on this court."

14   Peter Gibson LJ went on to hold that a decision of this court in *Lex Service plc v. Johns* [1990] 1 EGLR 92, which was subsequent to Galinski, had been decided per incuriam (at [26]). In Lex Service this court considered the relationship between section 23(1) of the LTA 1927 and section 7 of the Interpretation Act and held that non-receipt was not proved by its mere assertion. Therefore, for the purposes of section 23(1) and section 7, receipt was deemed to have been effected by reason of section 7. It was not a case where the issue, as in this case and as in *Galinski*, turned on whether time of service was on posting or on receipt. *Galinski* does not appear to have been cited, at any rate it is not mentioned in the judgments. In *Webber*, Peter Gibson LJ said of Lex Service :

"[25] It is clear, therefore, that both members of this court proceeded on the basis that section 7 applied to section 23. However, neither considered whether section 23 disclosed a contrary intention. The report of the case does not reveal any argument that there was a contrary intention disclosed by section 23. The applicability of section 23 appears simply to have been assumed by this court . . . "

15   The oddity is that section 7 does not appear to have been considered in *Galinski*. It can equally be said, therefore, that *Galinski* did not consider the question of whether section 23 disclosed a contrary intention. Nevertheless, this court in *Webber* considered that the question of contrary intention had been decided, as it were sub silentio, by *Galinski*. Thus at [29] in *Webber* Peter Gibson LJ said:

"For the reasons already given, it seems to me that the ratio of Galinski's case is inconsistent with that of the Lex Service case in so far as the Lex Service case decides that section 7 applies to section 23."

16   In coming to that conclusion it can be said that Peter Gibson LJ was also influenced by *Chiswell v Griffon Land and Estates Ltd* [1975] 1 W.L.R. 1181 (another, earlier, decision of this court), where section 7 had not been considered either, but Megaw LJ had observed (albeit obiter) that a notice sent by registered post, being one of the "primary methods laid down", was proof of sufficient service even if it were to be clearly established that it had gone astray and was never received; and by *Beanby Estates Ltd v Egg Stores (Stamford Hill) Ltd* [2003] 1 W.L.R. 2064, where section 7 was considered and Neuberger J reasoned that the point about the timing of service by registered post was strictly open but was not persuaded that he should depart from a previous decision by Smedley J in *Commercial Union Life Assurance Co Ltd v Moustafa* [1999] 2 EGLR 44, who had interpreted previous authority as pointing to the exclusion of section 7, and from the other indications in the jurisprudence. Peter Gibson LJ described Neuberger J's detailed judgment as helpful (at [32]).

17   Thus it was ultimately only in *Webber* that this court considered the relationship of section 23 of the 1927 Act and section 7 of the Interpretation Act, and held that the latter was excluded by the former, or at any rate that authority required such an answer. As to that, Peter Gibson LJ had begun his analysis with the comment that—

"[15] In the absence of authority, Mr Tanney's simple submission that section 23 contains nothing to exclude the applicability of section 7 would be well arguable. However, in the light of the authorities, several of them in this court, it seems to me impossible that Mr Tanney's first submission should prevail."

18   That of course was all in the context of section 23(1) of the 1927 Act and its express reference to "by sending it through the post in a registered letter addressed to him there". In the present case, there is no reference to registered post; but the argument that "by sending it by post ... " referred to in section 15(1) of the Act is again an alternative primary method of service is available and has been pressed on behalf of the respondent.

19   The question has been raised therefore whether this court is bound by either the decision or the reasoning in *Webber*, or whether section 15 of the Act is different in relevant respects from section 23(1) of the LTA 1927.

20   In that connection, none of the section 23 jurisprudence considers the position under section 15 of the Act (or other statutes). Section 15 was, however, considered in *Harpalani v Gray's Road Investment Limited* (HHJ Knight QC, unreported, 25 January 2010). Judge Knight there held that Webber was to be distinguished in the case of section 15 of the Act. He said that he saw "no logic" in section 15(1) requiring that the act of posting equates with service. Whereas

it was "understandable that service by registered letter transfers the risk of receipt to the recipient", there was no reference to registered post in section 15(1) (at para 23). Harpalani is the only prior case which has been discovered in which the present issue under section 15(1) has had to be decided. It also concerned a third surveyor's award which was posted before, but was received after, 14 days prior to a party's appeal to the county court.

21   It should be observed that section 7 has also been considered in connection with other statutes concerned with the service of documents by post. Thus the Housing Act 1985 contains provisions about notices in its section 176: section 176(3) states that "A notice under this Part may be served by sending it by post". (Section 176(4) also provides that a housing association may be served by its tenant "by leaving it [the notice] at, or sending it to, the principal office of the association ... ": which can permit the argument that, in the case of a landlord who is a housing association, there are two primary forms of service.) In *Terry v London Borough of Tower Hamlets* [2005] EWHC 2783 (QB) (Michael Supperstone QC, sitting as a deputy high court judge, unreported, 2 December 2005), the question was whether the claimant had proved serving a section 122 notice of his wish to exercise his right to buy prior to 26 March 2003, when the discount rules were changed. It appears to have been common ground that section 7 of the Interpretation Act applied. The claimant proved that his notice was posted by first class post on 6 March, and the defendant failed to prove non-receipt in the ordinary course of post (although it accepted having received it on 10 June 2003).

22   Section 99(1) of the Leasehold Reform, Housing and Urban Development Act 1993 provides that any notice required or authorised under the relevant part of that Act "may be sent by post". (There are again alternative provisions about methods for service in further sub-sections of section 99 in special cases.) In *Calladine-Smith v Saveorder Ltd* [2011] EWHC 2501 (Ch), [2012] L&TR 3 the dispute was between a tenant who had served a notice seeking to exercise his right to acquire a new lease on payment of a premium, and a defendant landlord who alleged that it had served a counter-notice. Section 7 was applied. The trial judge in the county court found that the counter-notice had been posted but not received, but that the claimant had not also proved that the letter had not been correctly addressed. Therefore the trial judge held that the notice was effective. On appeal, the claimant succeeded in reversing the decision: it was for the sender of the notice to prove correct addressing of the notice for the purposes of section 7, but it was sufficient for the addressee to prove that he had not received it, and that the claimant had done. *Webber* and other cases on section 23 were before the court. Morgan J contrasted section 23 with the provision in section 99(1) and said that it was agreed that section 7 of the Interpretation Act applied to that case (at para [8]).

23   Section 79(1) of the Commonhold and Leasehold Reform Act 2002 provides that a notice, which under section 79(1) of that Act has to be "given" to the landlord by a certain date, "may be sent by post". In *Moskovitz v 75*

Worple Road RTM Company Ltd [2010] UKUT 393 (LC), [2011] L&TR 4 George Bartlett QC, President, decided a disputed issue as to the application of section 7 to these provisions. The question was whether the defendant management company was entitled to manage 27 flats in a property owned by the claimant. The landlord said that the notice served by the company was served out of time, and succeeded, because it was held that, applying section 7, notice was not served, or "given", until it was deemed to have been received, viz in the ordinary course of post, not on posting.

24   It cannot be said, however, that the application of section 7 in these three cases was in issue on the ground that a "contrary intention" had been shown.

25   In this context I should also refer to section 17 of the Law of Property (Miscellaneous Provisions) Act 1994, which provides:

> "(1) Service of a notice affecting land which would be effective but for the death of the intended recipient is effective despite his death if the person serving the notice has no reason to believe that he has died.
>
> (2) Where the person serving a notice affecting land has no reason to believe that the intended recipient has died, the proper address for the purposes of section 7 of the Interpretation Act 1978 (service of documents by post) shall be what would be the proper address apart from his death."

It is submitted on behalf of the appellant that these provisions suggest that section 7 will at least generally apply to statutory provisions authorising or requiring the service of notices affecting land. I would accept that section 7 provides a general statutory code regarding sendings by post and that the statutory presumption is that it will apply—unless a contrary intention appears.

    . . .

36   In my judgment, the critical question for the interpretation of section 15(1) is, and must be, whether "the contrary intention appears" therein so as to exclude the otherwise statutory and thus mandatory application of section 7 of the Interpretation Act. No other question can have precedence in the working out of the issue as to the interrelationship of section 15(1) and section 7. For it is the intention of Parliament that, "unless the contrary intention appears", the concept of service by post is to be dealt with as provided for in section 7. It is as if section 7 (which goes back in its origins to very similar language in section 26 of the Interpretation Act 1889) provides the incorporated meaning of service by post in any statute which authorises or requires any document to be "served by post". Thus the critical question posed is to be resolved by imagining that section 7 is about to be written into the Act and then asking whether section 15 creates, either by its express language or by necessary implication, a situation where section 7 would be incompatible (contradictory or inconsistent).

37   It may be observed that section 7 is a complex alteration of the common law rule which requires receipt to effect service. Instead, section 7 deems service to be effected at the time the posted document would be received in the ordinary

course of the post. That presumption remains rebuttable, but the burden of doing so lies on the addressee. Another condition of the statutory refinement, however, is that the presumption only operates if a letter containing the document to be served has been properly addressed, pre-paid and posted ("by properly addressing, pre-paying and posting a letter containing the document"). The burden of proving that condition lies on the sender. The section seeks to answer various problems that might arise out of the posting of a letter, and to balance the interests of both the server and addressee. The ultimate formula, however, is to maintain that part of the common law rule which requires receipt, but to deem receipt to take place when would the letter be delivered in the ordinary course of post, subject to the right in the addressee to prove otherwise.

38   So, is there anything about the language or effect of section 15 which would be incompatible with section 7, if the latter section is imagined as potentially incorporated in the Act? Plainly, there is nothing in the express language which is any way incompatible. On the contrary, everything about that language points in the direction of service taking effect on receipt. First, that is the common law rule against which any statutory language must be measured. Secondly, the section speaks of service, which prima facie as a matter of language points to receipt ("A notice ... to be served ... may be served ... "). Thirdly, this requirement built into the concept of service is further emphasised by speaking about service on a person ("may be served on a person"). One would not naturally speak of serving a document on another person by long distance. Fourthly, section 15(1)(a) plainly requires such service on a person, for it speaks of the method "by delivering it to him in person". I find it hard to conceive that such a method does not involve receipt by that person. Of course, such a person may decline receipt by casting it from him, but if a notice is delivered by person to another person, I do not see that it can be properly said that the person to whom the notice is delivered can say that he has not received it.

39   I pass over section 15(1)(b) for the moment, which is the subject matter of dispute, and go on to section 15(1)(c) which concerns service on a body corporate. Section 15(1)(c) speaks of both delivery and, alternatively, use of the post. As for delivery, that plainly again contemplates receipt, albeit it suffices if delivery is to, ie receipt is by, "the secretary or clerk of the body corporate at its registered office". That language is necessary because a body corporate has to be represented by someone human and so the statute makes plain to whom the delivery of the document to be served is to be made. In the alternative case of post, the letter is likewise to be addressed to the secretary or clerk at the body corporate's registered office.

40   As for section 15(1)(b) and the latter part of section 15(1)(c), dealing with sending by post, there is again nothing in the express language which is in any way incompatible with section 7. Of course, once post is in issue, a question may always arise, as it cannot do in the case of personal delivery, as to whether it is the sending or the receiving by post which counts as service. However, even if there could be any doubt on that score against the background of the nature of

service in general, or in the context of the rest of section 15(1), section 7 is there to make it completely plain that, whether the expression used is "serve", "give", "send" or anything else, the concept of receipt remains the dominant concept, albeit there is a deemed receipt subject to proof otherwise. To my mind, there is nothing whatsoever in the express language of section 15 to suggest that section 7 is incompatible, so that "the contrary intention appears". I do not think that is disputed by Mr Nicholls.

41   So, the next question must be whether, in the absence of any express incompatible language, there is an implied exclusion of section 7. The respondent's submission, based on the section 23 jurisprudence, is that there is. The argument, as I understand it, is that because sending by post is one of the so-called primary methods of service, therefore it must be assumed that service is deemed to take place at the time of sending. I am unable to accept that argument as persuasive. Where the other primary methods contemplate service on the person to be served, I do not see why sending by post should be understood, either necessarily or even reasonably, to involve something short of that equivalent. I see that the issue may arise, but I do not see why section 7 does not answer it. It is there to answer it; and it does so by its refined reformulation of the common law. In the case of section 15(1)(c) and a body corporate, the sub-section tells us how the letter is to be addressed in order to meet the section 7 condition of "properly addressing" the addressee.

42   It seems to me that any other solution would be unreasonable, and therefore a highly improbable interpretation of the section. It would be unreasonable because it would be in disconformity with the common law, with the rest of section 15(1), and with the obvious intent of section 7 to provide the dominant presumption "unless the contrary intention appears". It would also be unreasonable because (a) the helpful code of section 7 would be lost; (b) a notice could be deemed served although established not to have been received, or received in time, which is essentially unfair, something which needs no authority to establish, but is in any event referred to in cases such as ex parte Saleem (at 453B/C, 458F/G, see above) or *FP (Iran) v Secretary of State for the Home Department* [2007] EWCA Civ 13, [2007] Imm AR 450 at paras [61] and [74]; (c) the short time limits of 14 days to be found in section 10(17) and elsewhere in the Act could be seriously eroded if time were to commence with the time of posting rather than the time of receipt (and there is nothing even to prevent a notice being consigned to the post with a second class stamp on it); and (d), in the case of a section 10(15) notice from a surveyor of his award, the document does not even come from a party. In saying this, I am conscious that the time limit for responding to notices by counter-notice extends to one month (see section 4(2)), and also that most of the notices for which the Act provides are notices between parties. However, there is nothing like the substantially longer notice periods for which the LTA 1954 speaks. I would also refer to the matters to which Mr Weekes has drawn attention (see at para [30] above) to the extent that they go beyond what is said here.

43   I would observe that section 15(2) fits into the same pattern, expressive of conformity with section 7. That deals with the special case of an addressee "as owner of premises". Such a person may "alternatively" be served by addressing the notice to such a person, describing that person as "owner" and also naming the premises, and delivering the notice "to a person on the premises". That also requires the receipt of the notice by a person at the premises concerned, although it may be not the person addressed as "owner" nor a person authorised to receive the notice on the owner's behalf. There is a further alternative built in, for, if no person "to whom it can be delivered is found there", the notice can be fixed "to a conspicuous part of the premises". In either case, the notice is delivered to a person at the premises or at least to the premises and affixed thereon. There is nothing here to suggest, by analogy, that, in the case of posting, mere posting without delivery to the addressed premises will suffice; nothing here which is incompatible with section 7. It is true that neither of these section 15(2) methods will necessarily involve the notice coming to the attention of the true owner of the premises, but nevertheless the statute is expressive of efforts to achieve service at the premises themselves of a notice addressed to their owner. Moreover, this alternative, which, unlike the section 15(1) alternatives, may not in fact result in the receipt of the notice by the addressee, is to my mind significantly dealt with in a separate sub-section from section 15(1).

44   Nevertheless, Mr Nicholls submits that the section 23 jurisprudence, at any rate by analogy, necessitates an answer to the same effect, namely that section 7 must be regarded as excluded. Mr Nicholls does not submit that this court is bound by *Webber* to reach the same answer with respect to section 15 of the Act, and accordingly he seeks to dispute any suggestion that Slade J proceeded on the basis that she was bound by the section 23 jurisprudence. Rather he submits that the section 23 jurisprudence, and in particular *Webber*, leads logically to the same result. I disagree. Section 23 is written in different terms from section 15, is to be found in a different statute, and the reasoning of its jurisprudence has developed in large part without consideration of section 7, even if ultimately in *Webber* the inference was drawn that section 7 was excluded.

45   Thus section 23 concerns a particular form of sending by post, namely by registered post. Moreover, it comes immediately after another alternative which refers to "leaving it for him at his last known place of abode in England or Wales". That is a method which may well not succeed in bringing about receipt by the addressee concerned. As for registered post, the advantage of this method of post is that (i) the day of posting will be recorded, (ii) the fact (and date) of delivery will be recorded, and (iii) if the letter cannot be delivered, it will be returned and the sender will be informed. Thus, if the letter goes astray or the addressee cannot be found, the sender will know, and ought to know more or less promptly, that that is so (see *Regina v County of London Quarter Sessions, Ex parte Rossi* [1956] QB 682 at 691/2). The same will be true of recorded delivery. In the case of the important notices with which the LTA 1927 and LTA 1954 are

concerned, it may well have been thought to be of particular importance that the validity of a timely service can be proved by the sender, in circumstances where, if there is no delivery, that will be soon established. In such a case, the sender of the notice can inform the addressee of his timeous posting and will also be in the position to prove his posting by the clear evidence available to him through the process of the registered post. Moreover, in the case of the LTA 1954, the addressee has two months in which to serve a counter-notice and four months to apply to the court for a new tenancy. In such circumstances, it can well be considered that a curtailment of that period for a few days, in the circumstances regulated by the process of registered post, is neither here nor there (see, albeit in the ECHR context, Neuberger J in *Beanby* at para [76]). The question of a sender of a section 23 notice who knows, through the post office, that his notice has not been received, but then does nothing to inform his addressee about the missing notice, seems to have been acknowledged by Neuberger J in *Beanby* (at paras [85]–[86]) as unattractive, but nevertheless as an example of "occasional harsh or unfair results" which may have to be tolerated in any system. For myself, I would hope that any server of a notice who knows that he has posted a valid notice and also knows that it has not been received and that the addressee therefore knows nothing about it and yet does nothing to inform addressee of the notice, would find his path strewn with difficulties. However, it seems to me that none of these considerations apply to the Act with which this appeal is concerned.

46   I have also been struck at how the section 23 jurisprudence has not proceeded so much by reference to section 7 of the Interpretation Act and its exclusion, as by reference to the construction of section 23 on its own terms. Thus in *Webber* this court reasoned that it was bound by this court's decision in *Galinski*, but *Galinski* did not consider section 7. In such circumstances, I do not consider that it would be appropriate to extend the reasoning applicable to section 23 of the LTA 1927 into a different statute, with different wording, by reference to which it cannot be said that section 7 is excluded on the basis that "the contrary intention appears".

47   Moreover, the "primary method of service" form of reasoning cannot explain those statutes which provide for simpler examples of permissive service by post, where it has been assumed that section 7 of the Interpretation Act applies. Mr Nicholls accepts that the "primary method of service" argument does not run to such cases. Yet, if a permissive form of service, viz sending by post, is authorised simpliciter, as in some at least of the statutes cited above, but is assumed, as in *Galinski* and *Webber* albeit in relation to the more complex wording in section 23, to apply for the benefit of the sender alone, then one could in theory arrive at a situation where section 7 is excluded simply because the statute concerned is assumed to grant a permissive method of service which goes beyond the common law, for the benefit of the sender, not the addressee. However, on the whole the assumption outside section 23 has been the other way around.

48   Slade J appears to have been influenced by the thought that "sending by post" can include registered post and recorded delivery (see at para [27] above) and that section 7 would add nothing to such forms of post. In this respect, and also in saying that the application of section 7 would deprive section 15(1)(b) and the latter part of section 15(1)(c) of any content, the judge appears to have thought that section 7 merely restates the common law. That, however, is not correct, for section 7 provides a code which goes beyond the common law. Moreover, section 7 can work well with a sending by registered post or recorded delivery: although in such a case it may have less to contribute in practice than in the case of a sending by ordinary post, proof of delayed or non delivery should be all the easier.

49   In the circumstances, there is no need to go on to consider the appellant's alternative submission that section 3 of the Human Rights Act may require section 15 of the Act to be interpreted in such a way as not to have the potential effect of destroying an effective right of appeal. It is sufficient to point out that analogous arguments failed in *Beanby* and in *Webber*, although it must be recognised that those cases were not considering a right of appeal. Moreover, although, on the alternative construction which has not persuaded me, the appellant in this case would have been just out of time, it could probably have managed to bring itself within the deadline, if its impact had been appreciated.

GENERAL ANTI-AVOIDANCE RULE[1]

Finance Act 2013

Part 5

General Anti-Abuse Rule

206 General anti-abuse rule

(1) This Part has effect for the purpose of counteracting tax advantages arising from tax arrangements that are abusive.

(2) The rules of this Part are collectively to be known as "the general anti-abuse rule".

(3) The general anti-abuse rule applies to the following taxes—

    (a) income tax,

    (b) corporation tax, including any amount chargeable as if it were corporation tax or treated as if it were corporation tax,

    (c) capital gains tax,

    (d) petroleum revenue tax,

    (e) inheritance tax,

    (f) stamp duty land tax, and

    (g) annual tax on enveloped dwellings.

207 Meaning of "tax arrangements" and "abusive"

(1) Arrangements are "tax arrangements" if, having regard to all the circumstances, it would be reasonable to conclude that the obtaining of a tax advantage was the main purpose, or one of the main purposes, of the arrangements.

(2) Tax arrangements are "abusive" if they are arrangements the entering into or carrying out of which cannot reasonably be regarded as a reasonable course of

---

[1] See new paragraph 29.1.5.3 above.

action in relation to the relevant tax provisions, having regard to all the circumstances including—

(a) whether the substantive results of the arrangements are consistent with any principles on which those provisions are based (whether express or implied) and the policy objectives of those provisions,

(b) whether the means of achieving those results involves one or more contrived or abnormal steps, and

(c) whether the arrangements are intended to exploit any shortcomings in those provisions.

(3) Where the tax arrangements form part of any other arrangements regard must also be had to those other arrangements.

(4) Each of the following is an example of something which might indicate that tax arrangements are abusive—

(a) the arrangements result in an amount of income, profits or gains for tax purposes that is significantly less than the amount for economic purposes,

(b) the arrangements result in deductions or losses of an amount for tax purposes that is significantly greater than the amount for economic purposes, and

(c) the arrangements result in a claim for the repayment or crediting of tax (including foreign tax) that has not been, and is unlikely to be, paid,

but in each case only if it is reasonable to assume that such a result was not the anticipated result when the relevant tax provisions were enacted.

(5) The fact that tax arrangements accord with established practice, and HMRC had, at the time the arrangements were entered into, indicated its acceptance of that practice, is an example of something which might indicate that the arrangements are not abusive.

(6) The examples given in subsections (4) and (5) are not exhaustive.

208 Meaning of "tax advantage"

A "tax advantage" includes—

(a) relief or increased relief from tax,

(b) repayment or increased repayment of tax,

(c) avoidance or reduction of a charge to tax or an assessment to tax,

(d) avoidance of a possible assessment to tax,

(e) deferral of a payment of tax or advancement of a repayment of tax, and

(f) avoidance of an obligation to deduct or account for tax.

209 Counteracting the tax advantages

(1) If there are tax arrangements that are abusive, the tax advantages that would (ignoring this Part) arise from the arrangements are to be counteracted by the making of adjustments.

(2) The adjustments required to be made to counteract the tax advantages are such as are just and reasonable.

(3) The adjustments may be made in respect of the tax in question or any other tax to which the general anti-abuse rule applies.

(4) The adjustments that may be made include those that impose or increase a liability to tax in any case where (ignoring this Part) there would be no liability or a smaller liability, and tax is to be charged in accordance with any such adjustment.

(5) Any adjustments required to be made under this section (whether by an officer of Revenue and Customs or the person to whom the tax advantage would arise) maybe made by way of an assessment, the modification of an assessment, amendment or disallowance of a claim, or otherwise.

(6) But—

(a) no steps may be taken by an officer of Revenue and Customs by virtue of this section unless the procedural requirements of Schedule 43 have been complied with, and

(b) the power to make adjustments by virtue of this section is subject to any time limit imposed by or under any enactment other than this Part.

(7) Any adjustments made under this section have effect for all purposes.

210 Consequential relieving adjustments

(1) This section applies where—

(a) the counteraction of a tax advantage under section 209 is final, and

(b) if the case is not one in which notice of the counteraction was given under paragraph 12 of Schedule 43, HMRC have been notified of the counter action by the taxpayer.

(2) A person has 12 months, beginning with the day on which the counter-action becomes final, to make a claim for one or more consequential adjustments to be made in respect of any tax to which the general anti-abuse rule applies.

(3) On a claim under this section, an officer of Revenue and Customs must make such of the consequential adjustments claimed (if any) as are just and reasonable.

(4) Consequential adjustments—

(a) may be made in respect of any period, and

(b) may affect any person (whether or not a party to the tax arrangements).

(5) But nothing in this section requires or permits an officer to make a consequential adjustment the effect of which is to increase a person's liability to any tax.

(6) For the purposes of this section—

(a) if the claim relates to income tax or capital gains tax, Schedule 1A to TMA1970 applies to it;

(b) if the claim relates to corporation tax, Schedule 1A to TMA 1970 (and not Schedule 18 to FA 1998) applies to it;

(c) if the claim relates to petroleum revenue tax, Schedule 1A to TMA 1970 applies to it, but as if the reference in paragraph 2A(4) of that Schedule to a year of assessment included a reference to a chargeable period within the meaning of OTA 1975 (see section 1(3) and (4) of that Act);

(d) if the claim relates to inheritance tax it must be made in writing to HMRC and section 221 of IHTA 1984 applies as if the claim were a claim under that Act;

(e) if the claim relates to stamp duty land tax or annual tax on enveloped dwellings, Schedule 11A to FA 2003 applies to it as if it were a claim to which paragraph 1 of that Schedule applies.

(7) Where an officer of Revenue and Customs makes a consequential adjustment under this section, the officer must give the person who made the claim written notice describing the adjustment which has been made.

(8) For the purposes of this section the counteraction of a tax advantage is final when the adjustments made to effect the counteraction, and any amounts arising as a result of those adjustments, can no longer be varied, on appeal or otherwise.

(9) Any adjustments required to be made under this section may be made—

(a) by way of an assessment, the modification of an assessment, the amendment of a claim, or otherwise, and

(b) despite any time limit imposed by or under any enactment other than this Part.

176

(10) In this section "the taxpayer", in relation to a counteraction of a tax advantage under section 209, means the person to whom the tax advantage would have arisen.

211 Proceedings before a court or tribunal

(1) In proceedings before a court or tribunal in connection with the general anti-abuse rule, HMRC must show—

    (a) that there are tax arrangements that are abusive, and

    (b) that the adjustments made to counteract the tax advantages arising from the arrangements are just and reasonable.

(2) In determining any issue in connection with the general anti-abuse rule, a court or tribunal must take into account—

    (a) HMRC's guidance about the general anti-abuse rule that was approved by the GAAR Advisory Panel at the time the tax arrangements were entered into, and

    (b) any opinion of the GAAR Advisory Panel about the arrangements (see paragraph 11 of Schedule 43).

(3) In determining any issue in connection with the general anti-abuse rule, a court or tribunal may take into account—

    (a) guidance, statements or other material (whether of HMRC, a Minister of the Crown or anyone else) that was in the public domain at the time the arrangements were entered into, and

    (b) evidence of established practice at that time.

212 Relationship between the GAAR and priority rules

(1) Any priority rule has effect subject to the general anti-abuse rule (despite the terms of the priority rule).

(2) A "priority rule" means a rule (however expressed) to the effect that particular provisions have effect to the exclusion of, or otherwise in priority to, anything else.

(3) Examples of priority rules are—

    (a) the rule in section 464, 699 or 906 of CTA 2009 (priority of loan relationships rules, derivative contracts rules and intangible fixed assets rules for corporation tax purposes), and

    (b) the rule in section 6(1) of TIOPA 2010 (effect to be given to double taxation arrangements despite anything in any enactment).

213 Consequential amendment

(1) Section 42 of TMA 1970 (procedure for making claims etc) is amended as follows.

(2) In subsection (2), for "(3ZB)" substitute "(3ZC)".

(3) After subsection (3ZB) insert—

"(3ZC) Subsection (2) also does not apply in relation to any claim under section 210 of the Finance Act 2013 (claims for consequential relieving adjustments after counteraction of tax advantage under the general anti-abuse rule)."

214 Interpretation of Part 5

In this Part—

"abusive", in relation to tax arrangements, has the meaning given by section 207(2) to (6);

"arrangements" includes any agreement, understanding, scheme, transaction or series of transactions (whether or not legally enforceable);

"the Commissioners" means the Commissioners for Her Majesty's Revenue and Customs;

"the GAAR Advisory Panel" has the meaning given by paragraph 1 of Schedule 43;

"the general anti-abuse rule" has the meaning given by section 206;

"HMRC" means Her Majesty's Revenue and Customs;

"tax advantage" has the meaning given by section 208;

"tax arrangements" has the meaning given by section 207(1).

215 Commencement and transitional provision

(1) The general anti-abuse rule has effect in relation to any tax arrangements entered into on or after the day on which this Act is passed.

(2) Where the tax arrangements form part of any other arrangements entered into before that day those other arrangements are to be ignored for the purposes of section 207(3), subject to subsection (3).

(3) Account is to be taken of those other arrangements for the purposes of section 207(3) if, as a result, the tax arrangements would not be abusive.

GOVERNMENT OF WALES ACT 2006

Legislative Competence of the National Assembly

Schedule 7

Acts of the Assembly[1]

Part 1

Subjects

1 Agriculture, forestry, animals, plants and rural development

Agriculture. Horticulture. Forestry. Fisheries and fishing. Animal health and welfare. Plant health.

Plant varieties and seeds. Rural development.

In this Part of this Schedule "animal" means—

(a) all mammals apart from humans, and

(b) all animals other than mammals;

and related expressions are to be construed accordingly.

Exceptions—

Hunting with dogs.

Regulation of scientific or other experimental procedures on animals.

Import and export control, and regulation of movement, of animals, plants and other things, apart from (but subject to provision made by or by virtue of any Act of Parliament relating to the control of imports or exports)—

(a) the movement into and out of, and within, Wales of animals, animal products, plants, plant products and other things related to them for the purposes of protecting human, animal or plant health, animal welfare or the

---

[1] See Chapter 4, Section 4 above.

environment or observing or implementing obligations under the Common Agricultural Policy, and

(b) the movement into and out of, and within, Wales of animal feedstuff fertilisers and pesticides (or things treated by virtue of any enactment as pesticides) for the purposes of protecting human, animal or plant health or the environment.

Authorisations of veterinary medicines and medicinal products.

2 Ancient monuments and historic buildings

Archaeological remains. Ancient monuments. Buildings and places of historical or architectural interest. Historic wrecks.

3 Culture

Arts and crafts. Museums and galleries. Libraries. Archives and historical records. Cultural activities and projects.

Exceptions—

Public lending right.

Broadcasting.

Classification of films, and video recordings.

Government indemnities for objects on loan.

Payments to Her Majesty's Revenue and Customs in respect of property accepted in satisfaction of tax, apart from property in which there is a Welsh national interest.

4 Economic development

Economic regeneration and development, including social development of communities, reclamation of derelict land and improvement of the environment. Promotion of business and competitiveness.

Exceptions—

Fiscal, economic and monetary policy and regulation of international trade.

Regulation of anti-competitive practices and agreements, abuse of dominant position and monopolies and mergers.

Intellectual property, apart from plant varieties.

Creation, operation, regulation and dissolution of types of business association.

Insolvency.

Product standards, safety and liability, apart from in relation to food (including packaging and other materials which come into contact with food), agricultural and horticultural products, [animals and animal products, seeds, fertilisers and pesticides (and things treated by virtue of any enactment as pesticides).

Consumer protection, including the sale and supply of goods to consumers, consumer guarantees, hire purchase, trade descriptions, advertising and price indications, apart from in relation to food (including packaging and other materials which come into contact with food), agricultural and horticultural products, animals and animal products, seeds, fertilisers and pesticides (and things treated by virtue of any enactment as pesticides).

Financial services, including investment business, banking and deposit-taking, collective investment schemes and insurance.

Occupational and personal pension schemes (including schemes which make provision for compensation for loss of office or employment, compensation for loss or diminution of emoluments, or benefits in respect of death or incapacity resulting from injury or disease), apart from schemes for or in respect of Assembly members, the First Minister, Welsh Ministers appointed under section 48, the Counsel General or Deputy Welsh Ministers and schemes for or in respect of members of local authorities.

Financial markets, including listing and public offers of securities and investments, transfers of securities, insider dealing and money laundering.

Telecommunications, wireless telegraphy (including electromagnetic disturbance), internet services and electronic encryption.

Postal services, post offices and the Post Office, apart from financial assistance for the provision of services (other than postal services and services relating to money or postal orders) to be provided from public post offices.

Generation, transmission, distribution and supply of electricity.

Energy conservation, apart from the encouragement of energy efficiency otherwise than by prohibition or regulation.

Coal, including mining and subsidence, apart from land restoration and other environmental matters.

Oil and gas.

Nuclear energy and nuclear installations—

(a) including nuclear safety and liability for nuclear occurrences;

(b) but not including disposal of very low level radioactive waste moved from a site requiring a nuclear site licence.

Units and standards of weights and measurement and the regulation of trade so far as involving weighing, measuring and quantities.

Industrial Development Advisory Board.

5 Education and training

Education, vocational, social and physical training and the careers service. Promotion of advancement and application of knowledge.

Exception—

Research Councils.

6 Environment

Environmental protection, including pollution, nuisances and hazardous substances. Prevention, reduction, collection, management, treatment and disposal of waste.

Land drainage and land improvement.

Countryside and open spaces (including the designation and regulation of national parks and areas of outstanding natural beauty).

Nature conservation and sites of special scientific interest.

Protection of natural habitats, coast and marine environment (including seabed).

Biodiversity. Genetically modified organisms. Smallholdings and allotments. Common land. Town and village greens. Burial and cremation, except coroners' functions.

7 Fire and rescue services and fire safety

Fire and rescue services. Provision of automatic fire suppression systems in newly constructed and newly converted residential premises. Promotion of fire safety otherwise than by prohibition or regulation.

8 Food

Food and food products. Food safety (including packaging and other materials which come into contact with food). Protection of interests of consumers in relation to food.

"Food" includes drink.

9 Health and health services

Promotion of health. Prevention, treatment and alleviation of disease, illness, injury, disability and mental disorder. Control of disease. Family planning. Provision of health services, including medical, dental, ophthalmic, pharmaceutical and ancillary services and facilities. Clinical governance and standards of health care. Organisation and funding of national health service.

Exceptions—

Abortion.

Human genetics, human fertilisation, human embryology, surrogacy arrangements.

Xenotransplantation.

Regulation of health professionals (including persons dispensing hearing aids).

Poisons.

Misuse of and dealing in drugs.

Human medicines and medicinal products, including authorisations for use and regulation of prices.

Standards for, and testing of, biological substances (that is, substances the purity or potency of which cannot be adequately tested by chemical means).

Vaccine damage payments.

Welfare foods.

Health and Safety Executive and Employment Medical Advisory Service and provision made by health and safety regulations.

10 Highways and transport

Highways, including bridges and tunnels. Street works. Traffic management and regulation. Transport facilities and services.

Exceptions—

Registration of local bus services, and the application and enforcement of traffic regulation conditions in relation to those services.

Road freight transport services, including goods vehicles operating licensing.

Regulation of the construction and equipment of motor vehicles and trailers, and regulation of the use of motor vehicles and trailers on roads, apart from—

183

(a) any such regulation which—

    (i) relates to schemes for imposing charges in respect of the use or keeping of vehicles on Welsh trunk roads ("trunk road charging schemes"), or

    (ii) relates to the descriptions of motor vehicles and trailers which may be used under arrangements for persons to travel to and from the places where they receive education or training, unless the regulation is the setting of technical standards for construction or equipment of motor vehicles or trailers which differ from the standards that would or might otherwise apply to them;

and

(b) regulation of the use of motor vehicles and trailers carrying animals for the purpose of protecting human, animal or plant health, animal welfare or the environment.

Road traffic offences.

Driver licensing.

Driving instruction.

Insurance of motor vehicles.

Drivers' hours.

Traffic regulation on special roads, apart from regulation relating to trunk road charging schemes.

Pedestrian crossings.

Traffic signs, apart from the placing and maintenance of traffic signs relating to trunk road charging schemes.

Speed limits.

International road transport services for passengers.

Public service vehicle operator licensing.

Documents relating to vehicles and drivers for purposes of travel abroad and vehicles brought temporarily into Wales by persons resident outside the United Kingdom.

Vehicle excise duty and vehicle registration.

Provision and regulation of railway services, apart from financial assistance which—

(a) does not relate to the carriage of goods,

(b) is not made in connection with a railway administration order, and

(c) is not made in connection with Regulation (EC) No 1370/2007 of the European Parliament and of the Council on public passenger transport services by rail and by road.

Transport security apart from regulation relating to the carriage of adults who supervise persons travelling to and from the places where they receive education or training.

Railway heritage.

Aviation, air transport, airports and aerodromes, apart from—

(a) financial assistance to providers or proposed providers of air transport services or airport facilities or services,

(b) strategies by the Welsh Ministers or local or other public authorities about provision of air services, and

(c) regulation of use of aircraft carrying animals for the purposes of protecting human, animal or plant health, animal welfare or the environment.

Shipping, apart from—

(a) financial assistance for shipping services to, from or within Wales, and

(b) regulation of use of vessels carrying animals for the purposes of protecting human, animal or plant health, animal welfare or the environment.

Navigational rights and freedoms, apart from regulation of works which may obstruct or endanger navigation.

Technical and safety standards of vessels.

Harbours, docks, piers and boatslips, apart from—

(a) those used or required wholly or mainly for the fishing industry, for recreation, or for communication between places in Wales (or for two or more of those purposes), and

(b) regulation for the purposes of protecting human, animal or plant health, animal welfare or the environment.

Carriage of dangerous goods (including transport of radioactive material).

Technical specifications for fuel for use in internal combustion engines.

11 Housing

Housing. Housing finance except schemes supported from central or local funds which provide assistance for social security purposes to or in respect of individuals by way of benefits.

Encouragement of home energy efficiency and conservation, otherwise than by prohibition or regulation. Regulation of rent. Homelessness. Residential caravans and mobile homes.

12 Local government

Constitution, structure and areas of local authorities. Electoral arrangements for local authorities.

Powers and duties of local authorities and their members and officers. Local government finance.

"Local authorities" does not include police authorities.

Exceptions—

Local government franchise.

Electoral registration and administration.

Registration of births, marriages, civil partnerships and deaths.

Licensing of sale and supply of alcohol, provision of entertainment and late night refreshment.

Anti-social behaviour orders.

Local land charges, apart from fees.

Sunday trading.

Provision of advice and assistance overseas by local authorities in connection with carrying on there of local government activities.

13 National Assembly for Wales

Complaints about Assembly members (including provision for and about an office or body for investigating such complaints and reporting outcome of investigations). Assembly Commission.

Salaries, allowances, pensions and gratuities for and in respect of Assembly members, the First Minister, Welsh Ministers appointed under section 48, the Counsel General and Deputy Welsh Ministers. Register of interests of Assembly members and the Counsel General. Meaning of Welsh words and phrases in Assembly Measures and Acts of the Assembly, in subordinate legislation made under Assembly Measures and Acts of the Assembly and in other subordinate legislation if made by the Welsh Ministers, the First Minister or the Counsel General. Private legislation in the Assembly. Financial assistance for political groups to which Assembly members belong. The Welsh Seal. Arrangements for the printing of Acts of the Assembly, of subordinate legislation made under

Assembly Measures and Acts of the Assembly and of other subordinate legislation if made by the Welsh Ministers, the First Minister or the Counsel General.

14 Public administration

Public Services Ombudsman for Wales. Auditor General for Wales. Audit, examination, regulation and inspection of auditable public authorities. Inquiries in respect of matters in relation to which the Welsh Ministers, the First Minister or the Counsel General exercise functions.

Equal opportunities in relation to equal opportunity public authorities. Access to information held by open access public authorities.

The following are "auditable public authorities" and "equal opportunity public authorities"—

(a) the Assembly,

(b) the Assembly Commission,

(c) the Welsh Assembly Government,

(d) persons who exercise functions of a public nature and in respect of whom the Welsh Ministers exercise functions,

(e) persons who exercise functions of a public nature and at least half of the cost of whose functions in relation to Wales are funded (directly or indirectly) by the Welsh Ministers, and

(f) persons established by enactment and having power to issue a precept or levy.

The following are "open access public authorities"—

(a) the Assembly,

(b) the Assembly Commission,

(c) the Welsh Assembly Government, and

(d) authorities which are Welsh public authorities, within the meaning of the Freedom of Information Act 2000 (c. 36).

Exception—

Regulation of the profession of auditor.

15 Social welfare

Social welfare including social services. Protection and well-being of children (including adoption and fostering) and of young adults. Care of children, young adults, vulnerable persons and older persons, including care standards. Badges for display on motor vehicles used by disabled persons.

Exceptions—

Child support.

Child trust funds, apart from subscriptions to such funds by—

(a) a county council or county borough council in Wales, or

(b) the Welsh Ministers.

Tax credits.

Child benefit and guardian's allowance.

Social security.

Independent Living Funds.

Motability.

Intercountry adoption, apart from adoption agencies and their functions, and functions of "the Central Authority" under the Hague Convention on Protection of Children and Co-operation in respect of Intercountry Adoption.

The Children's Commissioner (established under the Children Act 2004 (c. 31)).

Family law and proceedings, apart from—

(a) welfare advice to courts, representation and provision of information, advice and other support to children ordinarily resident in Wales and their families, and

(b) Welsh family proceedings officers.

16 Sport and recreation

Sport and recreational activities.

Exception—

Betting, gaming and lotteries.

17 Tourism

Tourism.

18 Town and country planning

Town and country planning, including listed buildings and conservation areas. Caravan sites.

Spatial planning. Mineral workings. Urban development. New towns. Protection of visual amenity.

Exception—

Development consent under the Planning Act 2008.

19 Water and flood defence

Water supply, water resources management (including reservoirs), water quality and representation of consumers of water and sewerage services. Flood risk management and coastal protection.

Exceptions—

Appointment and regulation of any water undertaker whose area is not wholly or mainly in Wales.

Licensing and regulation of any licensed water supplier within the meaning of the Water Industry Act 1991 (c. 56), apart from regulation in relation to licensed activities using the supply system of a water undertaker whose area is wholly or mainly in Wales.

20 Welsh language

Welsh language

Exception—

Use of the Welsh language in courts.

Part 2

General Restrictions

Functions of a Minister of the Crown

1 (1) A provision of an Act of the Assembly cannot remove or modify, or confer power by subordinate legislation to remove or modify, any precommencement function of a Minister of the Crown.

(2) A provision of an Act of the Assembly cannot confer or impose, or confer power by subordinate legislation to confer or impose, any function on a Minister of the Crown.

(3) In this Schedule "pre-commencement function" means a function which is exercisable by a Minister of the Crown before the day on which the Assembly Act provisions come into force.

2 (1) A provision of an Act of the Assembly cannot make modifications of, or confer power by subordinate legislation to make modifications of, any of the provisions listed in the Table below—

TABLE

Enactment Provisions protected from modification

European Communities Act 1972 (c. 68)	The whole Act
Data Protection Act 1998 (c. 29)	The whole Act
Government of Wales Act 1998 (c. 38)	Sections 144(7), 145, 145A and 146A(1)
Human Rights Act 1998 (c. 42)	The whole Act
Civil Contingencies Act 2004 (c. 36)	The whole Act
Re-Use of Public Sector Information Regulations 2005	The whole set of Regulations (S.I. 2005/1505)

(2) Sub-paragraph (1) does not apply to any provision making modifications, or conferring power by subordinate legislation to make modifications, of section 31(6) of the Data Protection Act 1998 so that it applies to complaints under an enactment relating to the provision of redress for negligence in connection with the diagnosis of illness or the care or treatment of any patient (in Wales or elsewhere) as part of the health service in Wales.

(3) Sub-paragraph (1), so far as it applies in relation to sections 145, 145A and 146A(1) of the Government of Wales Act 1998, does not apply to a provision to which sub-paragraph (4) applies.

(4) This sub-paragraph applies to a provision of an Act of the Assembly which—

(a) is a provision relating to the oversight or supervision of the Auditor General or of the exercise of the Auditor General's functions,

(b) provides for the enforcement of a provision falling within paragraph (a) or is otherwise appropriate for making such a provision effective, or

(c) is otherwise incidental to, or consequential on, such a provision.

3 A provision of an Act of the Assembly cannot make modifications of, or confer power by subordinate legislation to make modifications of, any provision of an Act of Parliament other than this Act which requires sums required for the repayment of, or the payment of interest on, amounts borrowed by the Welsh Ministers to be charged on the Welsh Consolidated Fund.

4 A provision of an Act of the Assembly cannot make modifications of, or confer power by subordinate legislation to make modifications of, any functions of the Comptroller and Auditor General or the National Audit Office.

5 (1) A provision of an Act of the Assembly cannot make modifications of, or confer power by subordinate legislation to make modifications of, provisions contained in this Act.

(2) Sub-paragraph (1) does not apply to the following provisions—

(a) sections 20, 22, 24, 35(1), 36(1) to (5) and (7) to (11), 53, 54, 78, 146, 147, 148 and 156(2) to (5);

(b) paragraph 8(3) of Schedule 2;

(c) any provision of Schedule 8, other than paragraphs 1(1) to (3), 2(2) to (4) and 3.

(3) Sub-paragraph (1) does not apply to any provision—

(a) making modifications of so much of any enactment as is modified by this Act, or

(b) repealing so much of any provision of this Act as amends any enactment, if the provision ceases to have effect in consequence of any provision of, or made under, an Act of the Assembly.

(4) Sub-paragraph (1) does not apply in relation to a provision to which paragraph 2(4) applies.

(5) But, subject to sub-paragraph (6), a provision to which paragraph 2(4) applies cannot modify, or confer power by subordinate legislation to modify, paragraph 3 of Schedule 8.

(6) Sub-paragraph (5) does not prevent the conferral of functions on a committee of the Assembly that—

(a) does not consist of or include any of the following persons—

   (i) the First Minister or any person designated to exercise functions of the First Minister,

   (ii) a Welsh Minister appointed under section 48,

   (iii) the Counsel General or any person designated to exercise the functions of the Counsel General, or

   (iv) a Deputy Welsh Minister, and

(b) is not chaired by an Assembly member who is a member of a political group with an executive role.

PART 3

EXCEPTIONS FROM PART 2

6 Functions of Ministers of the Crown

(1) Part 2 does not prevent a provision of an Act of the Assembly removing or modifying, or conferring power by subordinate legislation to remove or modify, any pre-commencement function of a Minister of the Crown if—

(a) the Secretary of State consents to the provision, or

(b) the provision is incidental to, or consequential on, any other provision contained in the Act of the Assembly.

(2) Part 2 does not prevent a provision of an Act of the Assembly conferring or imposing, or conferring power by subordinate legislation to confer or impose, any function on a Minister of the Crown if the Secretary of State consents to the provision.

7 Comptroller and Auditor General and National Audit Office

Part 2 does not prevent a provision of an Act of the Assembly modifying, or conferring power by subordinate legislation to modify, any enactment relating to the Comptroller and Auditor General or the National Audit Office if the Secretary of State consents to the provision.

8 Restatement

Part 2 does not prevent an Act of the Assembly—

(a) restating the law (or restating it with such modifications as are not prevented by that Part), or

(b) repealing or revoking any spent enactment, or conferring power by subordinate legislation to do so.

9 Subordinate legislation

Part 2 does not prevent an Act of the Assembly making modifications of, or conferring power by subordinate legislation to make modifications of, an enactment for or in connection with any of the following purposes—

(a) making different provision about the document by which a power to make, confirm or approve subordinate legislation is to be exercised,

(b) making provision (or no provision) for the procedure, in relation to the Assembly, to which legislation made in the exercise of such a power (or the instrument or other document in which it is contained) is to be subject, and

(c) applying any enactment comprised in or made under an Act of the Assembly relating to the documents by which such powers may be exercised.

CHALLENGES TO LEGISLATIVE COMPETENCE OF THE NATIONAL ASSEMBLY FOR WALES

Attorney General v National Assembly for Wales Commission
Supreme Court November 21, 2012 [2012] UKSC 53

Extracts from the judgment of Lord Neuberger (with whom Lords Clarke, Reed and Carnwath agreed)

7 The first Bill to be passed by the Assembly under its new power was the Local Government Byelaws (Wales) Bill 2012 ("the Bill"), the aim of which is to simplify procedures for making and enforcing local authority byelaws in Wales.

8 Certain provisions of the Bill, in particular section 6 and section 9 1, are intended to remove the need for the confirmation of byelaws by the Welsh Ministers or by the Secretary of State. Section 6 (through Part 1 of Schedule 1 to the Bill) refers to certain specific enactments ("the scheduled enactments") which currently require confirmation, and section 9 would empower the Welsh Ministers to add to those enactments.

9 The Secretary of State's consent to the inclusion of these two sections in the Bill was sought. She was prepared to agree to section 6 of the Bill ("section 6"), because she was content to give up her right to confirm byelaws made under the specific provisions identified in Part 1 of Schedule 1 to the Bill, but she was not prepared to agree to the inclusion of section 9 of the Bill ("section 9"). The Assembly nonetheless proceeded to pass the Bill with sections 6 and 9 in their original form. The Attorney General then referred to this court the question whether sections 6 and 9 were outwith the Assembly's legislative competence.

. . .

46 It is common ground between the original parties to this reference that section 6 is within paragraph 1 of Part 2 of Schedule 7 to the 2006 Act, in that it would have the effect of "remov[ing] . . . [a] pre-commencement function of a Minister of the Crown", namely the Secretary of State's role in confirming (or refusing to confirm) byelaws made under the statutory provisions which are (i) scheduled enactments, and (ii) provisions to which section 236(11) applies. On that basis the only issue is whether, as the

Counsel General contends (with the support of Mr Williams and the Attorney General for Northern Ireland), the section can be saved on the basis that, in so far as it would remove the pre- commencement function, it would be within paragraph 6(1)(b) of Part 3 of Schedule 7 to the 2006 Act, as it is "incidental to, or consequential on, [an] other provision contained in the [Bill]".

47 However, as already mentioned, the Attorney General for Northern Ireland challenges the otherwise agreed proposition that section 6 would remove the Secretary of State's confirmatory role under section 236(11) in relation to any scheduled enactments. He makes the point that section 1 only refers to the confirmatory powers of the Welsh Ministers, not to the Secretary of State's powers, and that no part of section 6 refers to his powers either.

48 In my view, this point highlights the way in which the Bill is structured, and, more importantly for present purposes, it tends to support the argument advanced by the Counsel General, namely that the removal by the Bill of the Secretary of State's power to confirm byelaws under section 236(11) is indeed "incidental to, or consequential on" one of the principal purposes of section 6 of the Bill, which is, as section 1 states, to remove the requirement for confirmation by the Welsh Ministers, as part of the overall streamlining and modernising of the way in which byelaws are made in Wales.

49 The answer to the question whether a particular provision in an enactment is "incidental to, or consequential on" another provision, obviously turns on the facts of the particular case. The answer may to some extent be a question of fact and degree, and it should turn on substance rather than form, although, of course, in any well drafted Bill, the substance will be reflected in the form, at least in relation to that sort of question.

50 Assistance on the point may be gleaned from what was said in this court in Martin v Most [2010] UKSC 10; [2010] SC (UKSC) 40, about paragraph 3(1)(a) of Schedule 4 to the Scotland Act 1998, which permits the Scottish Parliament to "modify the law on reserved matters" if, inter alia, the modification is "incidental to, or consequential on, provision made . . . which does not relate to reserved matters". There is a close similarity between those words and the words in paragraph 6(1)(b) of Part 3 of Schedule 7 to the 2006 Act, and the two provisions are concerned with similar material. However, they are found in different statutes, and one must therefore be wary of assuming that they have precisely the same effect, as context is so crucially important when interpreting any expression, perhaps particularly an expression as potentially fact-sensitive as "incidental to, or consequential on". Nonetheless, I consider that the approach adopted in that case is of assistance here.

51 In a brief passage at [2010] UKSC 10, paragraph 40, Lord Hope described a point as "important" in explaining why it was not "incidental

or consequential on provisions found elsewhere in the enactment". Lord Rodger described certain amendments as falling within paragraph 3(1)(a) of Schedule 4 to the Scotland Act 1998, if they "raise[d] no separate issue of principle", and were "safely stowed away in a schedule" in paragraph 93. He referred back to that observation at paragraph 128, where he described paragraph 3(1)(a) of Schedule 4 to the Scotland Act 1998 as "intended to cover the kinds of minor modifications which are obviously necessary to give effect to a piece of devolved legislation, but which raise no separate issue of principle". He contrasted them with other provisions which were "independent and deal with distinct aspects of the situation".

52 Section 6 of the Bill plainly is intended to have the effect of removing the need for confirmation by the Welsh Ministers of any byelaw made under the scheduled enactments. That is a primary purpose of the Bill, as is clear from reading the provisions quoted above, both in itself and for the purpose of streamlining and modernising the making of byelaws.

53 I consider that, applying the approach of Lord Hope and Lord Rodger in Martin v Most [2010] UKSC 10, the removal of the Secretary of State's confirmatory powers by the Bill in relation to the scheduled enactments would be incidental to, and consequential on, this primary purpose. In summary form, I reach this conclusion because of the following combination of circumstances, of which points (i) and (iv) are particularly telling. (i) The primary purpose of the Bill cannot be achieved without that removal, (ii) the Secretary of State's confirmatory power is concurrent with that of the Welsh Ministers, (iii) the confirmatory power arises from what is in effect a fall-back provision, (iv) the scheduled enactments relate to byelaws in respect of which the Secretary of State is very unlikely indeed ever to exercise his confirmatory power, (v) section 7 of the Bill reinforces this conclusion, and (vi) the contrary view would risk depriving paragraph 6(1)(b) of Part 3 of Schedule 7 to the 2006 Act of any real effect.

54 The first of these reasons is obvious. One of the streamlining and modernising purposes of the Bill would be undermined if the Secretary of State's confirmatory function remained in respect of any of the scheduled enactments. There would be no point in removing the Welsh Ministers' confirmatory function in relation to the scheduled enactments unless the Secretary of State's concurrent function was also disposed of. Indeed, the notion that the Assembly would intend to remove the Welsh Ministers' confirmatory function while retaining that of the Secretary of State is bizarre.

55 Secondly, there is attraction in the point that the Secretary of State's confirmatory function has become redundant on the basis that, as Lord Clarke put it, the enactment by the Assembly of section 6(1) amounted to a "blanket" confirmation in advance by the Welsh Ministers of any future byelaw made under the scheduled enactments, provided the procedures laid

down by sections 6(2) to (8) are complied with. While a blanket confirmation in advance of any byelaw cannot be a valid exercise of the Welsh Ministers' confirmatory function, the argument highlights the oddity of the Secretary of State's confirmatory power surviving the removal of the Welsh Ministers' confirmatory power.

56 Thirdly, there is the fact that the confirmatory function bestowed on the Secretary of State by section 236(11) is really a default function. The confirmatory function is only given to the Secretary of State if no other statute (including one passed after the 1972 Act) confers the function on any other body or person. To my mind, that feature tends to support the notion that it is not, to use Lord Hope's word in Martin v Most [2010] UKSC 10, paragraph 40, an "important" function. Thus, the point made by the Attorney General for Northern Ireland assists my conclusion.

57 Fourthly, and most crucially, the scheduled enactments concern byelaws whose nature is such that it would be for the Welsh Ministers, rather than the Secretary of State, to confirm them. This is because they are very much directed to local, small-scale (but important) issues. That point is strongly supported by the fact that it appears that, since the 1999 Order came into force, it has always been the Welsh Ministers, rather than the Secretary of State, who have exercised the confirmatory function in relation to byelaws made under any of the scheduled enactments. It seems to me that, in those circumstances, given the purpose of section 6, and the purpose of the Bill as explained in section 1, it would be positively perverse if the Secretary of State should retain the confirmatory function when the Welsh Ministers have disclaimed their confirmatory function. It was not suggested by Mr Swift that there were any circumstances envisaged by the Secretary of State in which she would wish to exercise her confirmatory function in relation to the scheduled enactments. In practical terms, this conclusion is supported by the fact that the only reason the Secretary of State did not consent to section 6 had nothing to do with the contents of that section or of Schedule 1, but with the inclusion of section 9 in the Bill.

58 Fifthly, as pointed out by Lord Reed, the provisions of section 7 of the Bill give some support for this conclusion. It establishes new concurrent powers in relation to byelaws (other than the scheduled enactments) which previously fell within section 236(11). Where subsections (11)(b) and (12) of section 7 apply, the confirmatory power of the Welsh Ministers is exercisable concurrently with that of the Secretary of State. This reinforces the argument that the Secretary of State's confirmatory function under section 236(11) is redundant as a result of the enactment of sections 6 and 7.

59 Finally, it is important, as the Counsel General argued, to arrive at a conclusion which gives a provision such as paragraph 6(1)(b) of Part 3 of Schedule 7 to the 2006 Act some real effect. It is difficult to think of circumstances in which it would have effect if it does not apply to section

6. Mr Swift suggested that, if it did not apply to section 6, it could still apply in a case where the Assembly abolished a statutory provision for byelaws altogether. I do not find that very persuasive. First, if he is right in the present case, it suggests that the provision can apply in a more extreme type of case than the present case, but not in the present case. Secondly, I am not convinced that it would be necessary to remove a power to confirm byelaws in relation to a given activity if the power to make byelaws in relation to that activity was abolished.

The central issue on this reference: section 9 of the Bill

60 Section 9 of the Bill would have the effect of enabling the Welsh Ministers to add to (and to subtract from) the scheduled enactments, which would then become subject to the section 6 procedure, rather than the section 7 procedure. As already explained, the crucial difference for present purposes between the two procedures is the requirement under section 7 for confirmation of the byelaw by Welsh Ministers and/or the Secretary of State or other Minister of the Crown (depending on the statutory provision under which the byelaw is made)—see, in particular, section 7(10) to (12).

61 The Attorney General's argument is that section 9 would "confer power" on the Welsh Ministers "by subordinate legislation to remove or modify . . . pre-commencement function[s] of a Minister of the Crown". Accordingly, he argues, by virtue of section 108(6)(a) of, and paragraph 1(1) of Part 2 of Schedule 7 to, the 2006 Act, the section is outside the legislative competence of the Assembly.

62 If section 9 is to be interpreted as giving the Welsh Ministers power to add to the scheduled enactments any enactment which gives the Secretary of State or another Minister of the Crown a confirmatory function in relation to byelaws, then I would accept that argument. However, there could be no objection to the section, if the scope of the power it would confer on the Welsh Ministers was limited to byelaws made under enactments which currently satisfy one of two requirements. Those requirements are that the enactment concerned (i) identifies the Welsh Ministers, and not a Minister of the Crown, as having the confirmatory power, or (ii) identifies a Minister of the Crown as having the confirmatory power, but the removal of that power would be "incidental . . . or consequential" within the meaning of paragraph 6(1)(b) of Part 3 of Schedule 7 to the 2006 Act. The basis for requirement (i) is self-evident, and the basis for requirement (ii) is the same as that for concluding that section 6 is within the legislative competence of the Assembly.

63 Although it is perfectly true that there are no express words in section 9 which limit its scope in this way, I am satisfied that it does have such a limited effect. That is because of the simple legal principle, identified by Lord Reed, embodied in the Latin maxim nemo dat quod non habet. Given that the jurisdiction of the Assembly is limited to removing, or delegating the power to remove, functions of Ministers of the Crown when the removal

satisfies the requirements of paragraph 6(1)(b) of Part 3 of Schedule 7 to the 2006 Act, the Assembly cannot confer a wider power on Welsh Ministers. Accordingly, the wide words of section 9 must be read as being circumscribed in their scope so as to render the section valid.

64 The same conclusion can be arrived at by invoking section 154(2) of the 2006 Act. It would not be permissible to invoke that statutory provision if it was inconsistent with the plain words of section 9. However, it would, in my view, be permissible to invoke it to limit the apparently unlimited and general effect of that briefly expressed section. Such an interpretation is consistent with the thrust of the Bill as a whole, and it does not conflict with any other provision in the Bill. And that point is reinforced by the fact that all the currently scheduled enactments satisfy requirements (i) or (ii).